The NOTTINGHAM COOKBOOK

Second Helpings

A celebration of the amazing food & drink on our doorstep.
Featuring over 45 stunning recipes.

The Nottingham Cook Book: Second Helpings

©2017 Meze Publishing. All rights reserved.

First edition printed in 2017 in the UK.

ISBN: 978-1-910863-28-2

Thank you to: Alex Bond, Alchemilla

Compiled by: Anna Tebble

Written by: Katie Fisher

*Photography by: Sam Bowles, Paul Carroll,
Vicky Elwick (www.stencil-agency.co.uk)*

*Additional photography: Darren Ciolli-Leach (Bar
Iberico), Matt Crowder, Xavier Buendia
(www.xdbphotography.com)*

Edited by: Phil Turner

Designed by: Paul Cocker, Marc Barker, Tom Crosby

PR: Kerre Chen

*Contributors: Faye Bailey, Joe Food, Rachel Havard,
Eleanor Keally, Sarah Koriba*

*Cover art: David Broadbent
(www.davidbroadbent.co.uk)*

me:ze
PUBLISHING

Published by Meze Publishing Limited
Unit 1b, 2 Kelham Square
Kelham Riverside
Sheffield S3 8SD
Web: www.mezepublishing.co.uk
Tel: 0114 275 7709
Email: info@mezepublishing.co.uk

Printed by Bell & Bain Ltd, Glasgow

FOREWORD

With over 19 years' experience of cooking in Michelin-starred restaurants, including Nottingham's illustrious Restaurant Sat Bains, Alex Bond fell in love with the thriving East Midlands food scene and decided to make his mark. Today he is head chef and owner of his latest venture in the city, the innovative Alchemilla restaurant on Derby Road.

A career working in kitchens can be nomadic; to climb the ladder, you have to do the leg work to get the experience, and that often means moving around to work in the best kitchens and train under the best chefs.

After stints working with some incredible chefs across the UK, I moved to Nottingham in 2008 to work at Sat Bains. Through his restaurant, Sat made the East Midlands a destination that people would travel to for amazing food: he upped the game and really opened my eyes to what was possible when you have a clear food philosophy and a bucket load of determination.

I realised that this was the region where I wanted to put down roots. Not only because the restaurant scene is no longer so London-centric; just look at the Waitrose Good Food guide and the latest Michelin Guide for proof, but also because this region is bursting with so much potential. We have a wealth of wonderful suppliers locally – Johnny Pusztai, for example, for incredible meat and poultry, or smaller artisan suppliers across the city – and the produce that this region generates is absolutely top notch. We also have vast untapped reserves of potential in our hedgerows and countryside; this summer the Alchemilla team foraged for sweet woodruff and elderflower which we have preserved, dried and turned into syrups to use in our cooking and cocktails.

Nottingham is such a creative and vibrant city. It has changed so much over the past five years and has so much potential: the 2023 European City of Culture bid; the development of the Creative Quarter; and the thriving independent food scene, with places such as Bar Iberico leading the way.

Nine years after moving to Nottingham, I am happily settled. My wife Anna and I have a beautiful daughter, whom we take to the allotment each week to learn about how things grow from one small seed. That's a great analogy for Alchemilla, which began with one small seed of an idea – to open my own restaurant one day – from which, plus years of hard graft and perseverance, came a bud, and from this, we hope to grow the best restaurant in the UK and make the East Midlands proud.

Alex Bond – Alchemilla

CONTENTS

Fall in love with
NOTTINGHAMSHIRE

If food is the fastest route to a person's heart, be rather careful in Nottingham – you might just fall in love. Our dining and drinking scene has never been so diverse, and at almost every turn you'll find streets embellished with restaurants, cafés and bars. Between the tempting waft of delicious aromas and the glimpses of intriguing interiors, it can be very hard to resist.

Aside from being incredibly enticing, perhaps what makes Nottingham's food scene truly unique is the city's own individual charm. Creative, ambitious, and certainly never dull, Nottingham has never been one to step in line. In fact, most of our defining moments throughout history originate from somebody deciding to sing to their own tune. From inventors to writers, rebels and eccentrics, Nottinghamshire is a county of innovation, and our culinary scene certainly reflects this.

Some of our most unique businesses have made their homes in historic sites around Nottingham, so it isn't hard to feel immersed in the city's history. The quirks and nuances of these structures make the experience all the more memorable, whether you're out for a pint or a three-course meal.

The airy bright windows of The Larder on Goosegate, for example, were built to display potions when it was the original Boots the Chemist in 1849. Today, passersby can see modern British and European cuisine being whipped up instead, topped with lashings of elegance and a brilliant view over Hockley.

The cells and bars of the old county prison at Shire Hall have been replaced with an intimate dining experience by Iberico World Tapas, complete with domed ceilings and elegant Moorish inspired design. Once you've eaten here, it's clear why the Michelin Guide chose Iberico to receive its Bib Gourmand accolade in 2017, recognising exceptional food at reasonable prices.

Alchemilla is another recent addition to the excellent fine dining options in Nottingham, and has taken up residence in the coaching house of a former lace merchant's property, disused for 176 years before its transformation. The restaurant is Alex Bond's brainchild, a chef who previously worked at the Michelin-starred Restaurant Sat Bains with Rooms.

It isn't just the buildings that represent the city's industrial past, however. Almost 700 caves have been discovered underneath Nottingham, shedding light on just how integral these curious subterranean spaces were to industry in days gone by. The sandstone caverns were hand carved beneath inns, streets and houses, and the perfect temperature for storing ale, leading to Nottingham beer being famed for

centuries. The tradition lives on in our great breweries, Castle Rock and Blue Monkey, or at small batch companies like The Angel Microbrewery, where the immense vessels are on show in the pub, so you can see ale in the making. One of England's oldest inns is nestled into the rock on which Nottingham Castle stands – Ye Olde Trip to Jerusalem is a wonderfully historic spot to enjoy classic pub grub and carefully chosen local ales.

In the lush countryside surrounding the city, household favourites, local delicacies and delicious classics of the future are being created using locally sourced ingredients and much love and care. Not far from where the fruit was first grown in the 19th century, the Bramley apple is picked, pulped and juiced by Starkey's Fruit at the family-run Southwell orchard and fruit farm. Further south, a traditional method for making Stilton has been handed down for over 100 years at the famous Colston Bassett Dairy, making it one of the only places in the country to produce the authentic taste of the 'king of cheese'. If you're passing Retford, a diversion to Thaymar Ice Cream, Farm Shop & Tea Room is a must. The award-winning Elderflower and Gooseberry ice cream is just one of 35 flavours created on site. A more recent addition to these creative inventors is Sauce Shop, a family business that takes making delicious sauce seriously, and makes seriously good sauce.

But it's not all about what's right on the doorstep for Nottingham nosh – the array of modern international cuisine in the county will beckon those with a taste for the exotic! Dine in a tuk-tuk at Zaap Thai, dip into a zingy curry at renowned Indian restaurant MemSaab, or enjoy the rustic tapas of Beeston's The Frustrated Chef.

If it's a bit of good old British grub you're after though, there's still plenty of choice. The Cod's Scallops have made waves with their delicious fish and chips, offering a fabulous range of fresh seafood to eat in or cook at home. For a taste of English tradition, why not try a Crafternoon Tea at Debbie Bryan, the gorgeous creative studio keeping our textile heritage alive in The Lace Market?

Back in the 21st century, herbivores and carnivores can at last dine peacefully together in many of Nottingham's eateries. The menu at the award-winning Annie's Burger Shack is famed for its huge selection of juicy burgers catering for veggies, vegans and meat lovers, and likewise at The Angel Microbrewery, where some say the beer battered halloumi and chips is better than the real thing.

But all of this culinary expertise is no longer reserved purely for professionals – if you have picked up this book then you're probably already tempted to go wild in the kitchen and cook up a delicious storm. If starting from scratch isn't your thing, seek out one of our brilliant farm or speciality shops, many of which are mentioned in this book, to find inspiration and the best quality local produce.

For an extra helping hand, there are various cookery classes available at venues across the county where enthusiasts, complete beginners, and anyone in between can pick up tips and tricks to take their foodie habit one step further. Having been satisfying coffee lovers of Nottingham for the past few years, 200 Degrees Coffee Roasters are now revealing how to master the perfect latte at their Barista School, whilst at The Welbeck Estate's prestigious School of Artisan Food there are oodles of courses covering techniques and specialities such as fermentation, patisserie and chocolate making.

Now you know what's out there, take a little time to relax with a drink or a snack, and browse through this enticing collection of stories and recipes from Nottingham's most talented and diverse culinary creatives.

From bean TO BARISTA

Nottingham-based 200 Degrees Coffee Roasters create, sell and ensure the longevity of their artisan product from their Meadow Lane roastery, inviting coffee shops and Barista School. For coffee lovers, this is not one to be missed…

200 Degrees Coffee owners Tom Vincent and Rob Darby met at Nottingham University, and graduated from their strong interest in real ale to a passion for great coffee. Having struggled to find the perfect brew for their customers whilst working in the hospitality industry, Rob and Tom decided the easiest way to achieve their goal would be to simply roast the beans themselves. The name of the company they created, incidentally, refers not only to the temperature, in degrees Celsius, that they roast their beans at (bigger companies tend to go for a more ferocious heat) but also to the temperature, in degrees Fahrenheit, at which coffee is ideally brewed.

200 Degrees has since gathered a group of like-minded coffee enthusiasts in the roastery, two coffee shops and a barista school found at various locations around Nottingham, with three other schools and four more shops further afield. The school offers a variety of courses designed to encompass all skill levels, from amateur to professional, and the shops all have their own distinct feel, but are united by a focus on the quality of the coffee. For Tom, the coffee shops are a great way to showcase their product, but are also cosy places designed to invite relaxation.

The house blend is always available in the shops, but the guest single origin changes weekly, depending on what's in production at the roastery. The team follow coffee seasons and harvests, sourcing their beans from all over the world to truly reflect the best available flavours. Around one ton of the end product is sold wholesale per week, roasted to order and sent off with expert knowledge packed into every bag. 'Tim the Coffee Guy' travelled around New Zealand to gather his in-depth knowledge, turning an interest into a vocation in the meantime, and Mike Steele – 'Master of the Roast and Blend' – is on a mission to create perfection and deliver the ultimate cup of coffee.

The amount of care taken to select the ingredients and methods used at 200 Degrees is genuinely impressive. Add to this the undeniable passion (and in their own words, geekiness) of the team who work in the shops, the roastery and the schools and you have a combination that produces authentic experiences – whether that's learning, drinking or home-brewing – every time. To coffee lovers who haven't tried 200 Degrees Coffee Roasters' artisan product yet: wake up and smell it!

200°
COFFEE

ROAST HOUSE
COFFEE SHOPS
BARISTA SCHOOL
SUBSCRIBE ONLINE

200degs.com

Barista School

QUICHE of
the DAY

Dill, Red Chilli
Leek, Fennel
w feta £3.25

BOWL of
3 SALADS

£4.50

Side Salad

£2.75

SOUP of
the DAY

PARSNIP, CELERY
ROAST PEPPER,
CINNAMON
CREAM £4.50

200 Degrees Coffee Roasters
OUR FAVOURITE BREWS

Coffee can be brewed and enjoyed in numerous ways, all of which bring out different flavours and create distinct experiences. We've chosen two of our favourite brew methods based on how our experts at the roastery do it, both of which produce excellent coffee with ease.

First up, the Chemex method. Perfect for a lazy Sunday, when you can afford the time to appreciate the process and the delicate nature of the brew. Paying that little bit more attention to detail here will be absolutely worth it.

Ingredients

17g coffee (medium to coarse grind)

300ml hot water (use 30 seconds after boiling)

Equipment needed

3-cup Chemex

Chemex filter papers

Kettle

Scales

Grinder

Timer

Method

Start by placing the folded Chemex filter paper into the Chemex, with the thick side against the spout. Wet the filter evenly, using hot water so the Chemex is preheated, then discard the water.

Place the Chemex on the scales, add the coffee, and level it out in the Chemex.

Start the timer, add 120ml of the boiled water in a circular motion and wait for 35 seconds. Now, add 60ml of water. When timer reaches 1 minute 30 seconds, add 60ml of water. When the timer reaches 2 minutes add the final 60ml of water. When all the water has drained through, your coffee is ready. In total, the brewing time should be about 3 minutes and 30 seconds. Remove and discard the filter before pouring the coffee into cups or mugs and serving.

Next up, the Aeropress method. This is a daily ritual for many, who want a quick coffee with little fuss but maximum flavour and quality. The Aeropress is readily available and comes with everything you need to get started (minus the coffee, but we can sort that!).

Ingredients

15g coffee (medium grind)

240ml hot water (use 30 seconds after boiling) Aim for a 1 minute and 40 second total brew time

Equipment needed

Aeropress

Aeropress filter papers

Aeropress Paddle

Kettle

Scales

Grinder

Timer

Jug

Method

Place the paper filter inside the filter cap, then wet the filter and set aside for later. Create a seal between the top and bottom of the Aeropress about a centimetre in. Place the Aeropress on the scales with the cap side facing up.

Weigh the coffee into the Aeropress, start the timer and add 100ml of water. Stir five times with the Aeropress paddle. At 30 seconds, add the remaining 140ml of water, stir five times and place the filter on the top, making sure to lock it into place.

At 1 minute 10 seconds, flip the Aeropress over onto a jug and plunge for 30 seconds. Stop plunging when you hear a hiss of air. The coffee is now ready to serve. Make sure to discard the coffee grounds and the used filter by carefully removing the filter cap over a bin. Now rinse the Aeropress with hot water so it's ready for the next coffee-making.

Last but not least, here are our top tips for coffee lovers:

Look for a 'roasted on' date to ensure your coffee is the freshest it can be.

Keep in a cool, dry place (avoid the fridge and freezer).

Ideally grind your coffee just before use, for ultimate freshness.

Pure ALCHEMY

With Alchemilla, Alex Bond aims to create an embodiment of relaxed fine dining, and despite being a newcomer to the city, this restaurant is already one of Nottingham's most exciting places to eat out.

Nottingham's brand new restaurant Alchemilla, named after a plant that is known for collecting the purest water on its leaves historically used in healing potions, might be best described as 'pared down' as regards the menu, the interior and the ethos of the dining experience – but this doesn't mean that every element you encounter isn't of the highest possible quality. Head chef and owner Alex Bond has thrown himself into this venture with passion but also with precision, wanting to concentrate on ensuring that everything the restaurant creates is outstanding.

Alex recognises the importance of consistency, whether cooking the five course menu for two, or the ten course menu for four tables, which has clearly set an impressive standard, with the restaurant already booked up months in advance. For all this may sound like a prestigious evening out solely for the likes of tuxedo-wearing patrons, the opposite is in fact true. Alchemilla is about accessibility and comfort as well as amazing food – Alex places no restrictions on attire for diners, plays music he likes through the restaurant speakers which might be soul, funk, hip hop or jazz depending on the day, and generally eschews the 'frills' that you might expect to accompany fine dining.

Continuing in that vein, Alchemilla offers a distinguished wine list, but also serves beer and cocktails alongside the three tasting menus. The ingredients for every dish on these menus are British, meaning the produce is sourced only from the UK and according to the seasons, because, as Alex puts it, cooking this way is 'just logical' in terms of flavour, quality and finances. There is a bias towards vegetable-based dishes due to Alex's love of a challenge in the kitchen, and the fact that in his eyes, meat simply doesn't have to be the main event. He enjoys seeing people's preconceptions change, and also being able to price a visit to his restaurant fairly.

Contrast is a key feature at Alchemilla, and nowhere is that more evident than in the interior of the building that houses the restaurant. Empty for 150 years before the renovation team moved in to complete essential works and not much else, the old coaching house has been given a new lease of life whilst retaining all its original character. The result is a minimal space, raw but refined, that reflects Alex's fuss-free approach to the whole project. A walled roof garden is currently in progress, adding a touch more intrigue to this very young, but very unique venture – we can't wait to see where Alchemilla goes from here.

EVENING BAR WINE

Alchemilla

Alchemilla
BLACK PUDDING, SMOKED EEL, BEETROOT

The key to great black pudding is fresh blood, and at the restaurant we use braised pigs head which results in nice, large pieces of meat which go in the pudding as well.

Preparation time: 1 ½ hours | Cooking time: approx. 5 ½ hours | Serves 12

Ingredients

For the black pudding:

3g crushed garlic

80g diced leek

40g butter

13g salt

7g allspice

1g each of ground cinnamon, ginger, cumin, star anise and nutmeg

100g shallot compote

1 litre blood

90ml double cream

750g cooked pig's head or braised pork shoulder

For the smoked eel and oil:

1 fresh eel

Apple wood chips

100ml grapeseed oil

For the beetroot:

600ml beetroot juice

5g agar agar

50g pickling liquor

To serve:

Blackberry vinegar

Wild rice

Unagi sauce

Method

Start by making the black pudding. Sweat the garlic and leek in butter. Add the salt and all the spices, and cover the pan with cling film to steam the mixture for approximately 5 minutes until the leeks are tender. Add the shallot compote, then the blood and cream, and warm to 40°c.

Pour the mixture over the braised pig's head or pork shoulder on a lined tray. The meat should be shredded into roughly 2cm x 2cm pieces and scattered across the bottom of a cling filmed tray which is then sat in a larger tray of water and tin foiled. Cook in preheated oven at 80°c until the core temperature reaches 85°c, then refrigerate for later.

Next, cold smoke the eel using the apple chips until delicately smoked (alternatively you could buy from a reputable supplier). Prepare the eel by cutting into pieces half the size of a playing card and setting these aside. Place the skin and bones in the grapeseed oil and warm to 36°c and keep at that temperature for 30 minutes. Pass the mixture through a sieve and retain the flavoured oil for later.

Boil 500ml of the beetroot juice with the agar agar and set. Once set, blend the juice with the pickling liquor to a ketchup consistency. Reduce the remaining beetroot juice by half and mix with the eel oil and a dash of blackberry vinegar to make the dressing.

Lastly, deep-fry the wild rice at 220°c, drain on a cloth or kitchen paper and season to taste.

To serve

Portion the black pudding and pan fry until crispy on one side. Place a piece of the eel on top, brush with unagi sauce and glaze under the grill. Arrange the black pudding and eel slices on the plate, pipe some of the ketchup on top of the eel, dress with the eel oil and beetroot juice emulsion, and finally sprinkle with puffed wild rice to serve.

A new
LEASE OF LIFE

Angel Freehouse and Microbrewery has turned The Old Angel Inn into a
wonderfully traditional, relaxed and accessible place to eat,
drink and catch live music in Nottingham's Lace Market area.

Benjamin Rose had been harbouring the idea of starting his own microbrewery for years, having lived in Germany where all the pubs were brewing their own beer, so when the premises of The Old Angel Inn came up it didn't take him long to jump at the opportunity. The building itself is over 400 years old, so despite the presence of a pub on the site for half of that time, it still needed extensive refurbishment. That's not to say Benjamin and his team have created a blank canvas; the owner and founder was keen to let the incredible piece of architecture speak for itself and has retained as much of the character of the place as possible.

The bar, eating area and kitchen came first and have been open to the public for just under a year and a half, offering relaxed dining and plenty of local ales for all tastes and requirements. The menu has a 'carnivores' side versus an 'herbivores' side, so there are extensive options for vegans and vegetarians – which include all the ales on the bar – as well as meat-eaters who can enjoy organic produce sourced from the nearby Peak District. Sustainable and ethical farming is important to Angel Microbrewery, as is the high quality, fresh food that the chefs create as a result.

As far as the bar line-up is concerned, there are no set rules about what to feature, though in the future Benjamin aims to have four of their own and four guest beers showcased at a time. The microbrewery has been up and running since the beginning of 2017, and so far two of the half dozen recipes the team have developed have made public appearances – the American 'Yippee Aye Ay IPA' for example has gone down so well it recently sold out! Another recent addition to the venue is the renovated upstairs space, which has a fascinating and potted history having been a brothel and a chapel (at different times, we assume) and since the end of 2016, a renowned music venue, with local acts as well as bigger names regularly playing gigs in the double height space.

With his easy-going, unpretentious philosophy on all aspects of the freehouse and microbrewery, Benjamin has created a great venue, eatery and bar as well as upholding Nottingham's long-standing affinity with beer brewing in the tradition and spirit of the building Angel Microbrewery inhabits. With just a year and a half behind it, we look forward to seeing Angel's reincarnation go from strength to strength.

TODAY'S PIES

HERBIVORE
Smokey Chickpea and Tofu. Served with chips or mash, Seasonal greens and onion gravy. £8.50 (Vg)

CARNIVORE
Beef, Ale and Stilton
Served with mash or chips, Seasonal greens and gravy £10

Angel Microbrewery
VEGAN STICKY TOFFEE CHEESECAKE

There are lots of vegan options on the menu at Angel Microbrewery, including the ales, so this indulgent cheesecake is the perfect way to round off a meal there. It's also easy to make at home, and the natural sweetness of the dates beautifully complements the caramel flavours of the sauce.

Preparation time: 15 minutes | Cooking time: 40 minutes | Serves 4

Ingredients

For the base:

300g digestive biscuits

100g dairy-free margarine

For the topping:

450g plain tofu (squeeze to remove water)

255g dairy-free cream cheese

160g icing sugar

250g dates

300ml water

1 tsp bicarbonate of soda

For the sauce:

250ml soy cream

200g brown sugar

Method

Preheat the oven to 180°c. Blend together the biscuits and margarine, then tip the mixture into a small cheesecake tin and press it down to form a base. Bake for 10 minutes or until golden brown.

Next, put the dates, water and bicarbonate of soda into a small saucepan and cook over a low heat until the dates are softened. Separate the dates and liquid using a sieve, and set both parts aside.

In a mixing bowl, blend together the tofu, icing sugar and cream cheese until smooth. Add the dates and blend again for 20 seconds. Once the biscuit base has cooled, pour this mixture over the top and smooth with a spoon. Bake at 180°c for 20 minutes, then allow the cheesecake to cool before slicing and serving.

For the sauce, put the leftover date liquid, soy cream and brown sugar into a small saucepan and whisk together. Set over a low heat until the mixture boils. Allow to cool, then drizzle over a slice of cheesecake to enjoy.

Sunny SIDE UP

Cultivating an old-fashioned US restaurant vibe against the backdrop of the historic Lace Market area, Annie's Burger Shack brings the best of two American staples – authentic burgers and breakfasts – to Nottingham.

Already famous for a hefty menu of real American-style burgers with culinary twists, Annie's started to break new ground, as well as a whole lot of eggs, with the introduction of the 'Four Corners' breakfast menu in early 2016. Dishes are inspired by favourites from The Pacific Northwest, New England, The Southwest and The South – think Dixieland Grits (very traditional Southern fare), Boston Baked Beans and Huevos Rancheros, amongst many more.

Owner Anmarie Spaziano – better known as Annie – grew up in Rhode Island, down the road from Providence, where the first ever American diner opened to the public from a repurposed horse-drawn wagon. When she moved to the Midlands in 1994, Annie discovered a love of real ale, so when it came to establishing her business combining the two seemed obvious, and in 2009 Annie's Burger Shack and Freehouse was born. Annie describes her highly successful venture as the 'best of both worlds' coming together – cask ale and handcrafted burgers are a harmonious partnership indeed. Even the architecture of the Lace Market reminds her of home, and Annie has taken inspiration for the food and décor from her New England roots accordingly.

Though burgers might be synonymous with fast food to some, Annie's is all about the dining experience. Even before the move to the beautiful and spacious Lace Market premises, all the food was cooked to order from scratch by Annie and served from the pub kitchens of the Old Angel, and later the Navigation on Canal Street. All of Annie's burgers are made on site daily and amazingly, every burger and breakfast option can be made vegan, veggie or meaty depending on the customer's preference. If that's not dedication, we don't know what is!

The relaxed atmosphere allows guests time to enjoy the surroundings. Particular features of interest include the bar, which is panelled with rounds of reclaimed wood from Sherwood Forest, and the childhood memorabilia adorning the walls belonging to – you guessed it – Annie herself. Her intercontinental loyalties have provided the Nottinghamshire public with a feast for the eyes and the stomach – with breakfast, burgers and beers on offer we could quite happily stay all day.

Annie's Burger Shack

EASY PORTLAND STUFFED FRENCH TOAST WITH VANILLA CREAM CHEESE & MIXED BERRY COMPOTE

This is a very popular dish that I love to serve to friends as a late and lazy breakfast. Depending on who you're cooking for, it's great with vegan, veggie, or meaty Lincolnshire or American style sausages – the sage in these works extremely well with the sweetness of the berries and maple syrup.

Preparation time: 15 minutes | Cooking time: 20 minutes | Serves 6

Ingredients

For the compote:

1 kg frozen mixed berries, defrosted

450g granulated sugar

Knob of butter (optional)

For the French toast:

2 large loaves tiger bread (day old is best)

560g cream cheese

1 tbsp vanilla extract or 1 vanilla pod, scraped

175g granulated sugar

6 eggs

1 tbsp cinnamon

Splash of milk

To serve:

Icing sugar

Butter

Maple syrup

Sausages or bacon (optional)

Method

The night before, take the berries out of the freezer to defrost. If the bread is fresh, slicing the loaves and leaving them in a paper bag to dry out the middles makes it easier to work with the following day.

Pour the defrosted berries, along with all their juice, into a saucepan and bring to a gentle simmer over a medium heat. Stir in the sugar, add the butter if using, and turn the heat down to medium-low. Keep an eye on the compote whilst making the French toast and stir frequently to avoid it sticking. The mixture should gradually reduce and become thick enough to coat the back of a spoon.

Next cut the bloomers into a dozen thick, even slices of about 5cm thickness. Carefully cut a pocket in each slice, starting from the front of the crust and slicing inwards. Leave at least a 2cm gap between the pocket and the edges of the slice so the filling can't leak out.

In a medium-sized bowl, beat the cream cheese with the sugar and vanilla until fully combined. Take a dessert spoon and carefully fill each pocket with roughly two tablespoons of the mixture, being careful not to split the bread.

Now preheat a frying pan over a medium heat, and grease just before use. Crack the eggs into a separate bowl, add the cinnamon and a splash of milk if using, and beat together. Dip both sides of the filled bread in the egg mixture, leaving it to soak for a few seconds on each side. Then melt the butter in the frying pan and fry each piece of French toast gently for 4-5 minutes, turning halfway through cooking, until nicely browned and warmed through.

To serve

Arrange two of the French toasts criss-crossed on a plate, and use a sieve to dust with icing sugar. Add a small knob of room-temperature butter on top and pour some maple syrup over the French toast. Spoon the berry compote over whilst it's hot, place some sausages or crispy American-style streaky bacon on the side if desired, and serve immediately.

For a vegan and vegetarian alternative to this recipe, simply replace the eggs with 375ml almond milk, leave out the extra splash of milk, use vegan cream cheese and a non-dairy spread instead of butter. Serve with vegan sausages and/or vegan bacon if desired.

They're ON A ROLL

Set in an unassuming suburb of Nottingham but rising steadily through the baking halls of fame. 'Keep it simple, do it well' is the motto behind the whirlwind success of The Bakehouse.

Husband and wife team Craig and Rosea Poynter opened The Bakehouse just ten months ago, but their bakery / café / micro-pub is already a fixture of the community, and has gained county-wide and now national recognition. It was a runner-up for the Nottinghamshire Post's 2017 Best New Venue award, and the wholemeal bread recently picked up a National Great Taste award, making it the only bakery in Nottinghamshire to win one of these coveted recognitions for bread in 2017.

These accolades are hard-won and well-earned, considering that Craig and Rosea have undertaken this journey at the same time as starting a family – their son was just 4 months old when they picked up the keys, and is now so well-known at The Bakehouse that customers named a beer specially created for the café by Welbeck Abbey Brewery after him: Baker's Boy.

That partnership with the Welbeck Estate is just one of many connections The Bakehouse has forged with the local community. The retail section stocks products from Sauce Shop and Bluebird Tea Company, and Rosea's strong sense of social responsibility has led to all the bakery's unsold bread being donated to local refugee and homeless charities at the end of each day. No wonder the Spirit of Sherwood award counts among The Bakehouse's recent accolades, voted for by local people in recognition of a business that really gives back to the county.

It shouldn't come as a surprise that The Bakehouse has people literally knocking on the door to work with them – their talented head chef George approached them, as did their invaluable baker Chris who was thrilled to join the venture in its earliest stages (The Bakehouse was still a building site when he knocked on the door) having worked through an era of supermarket takeovers, and keen to reignite his passion for real baking using great ingredients and traditional methods.

Even more exciting times lie ahead for Craig, Rosea and little Fred as their second premises, purchased last month, gets set up for wholesale production. Despite their relative fame and success, The Bakehouse is at heart a humble business, passionate about honest, high quality food as well as provision for the community around them. Craig and Rosea's refusal to compromise on provenance, sustainability, taste and quality has been well rewarded, and with all the time and love invested, their success is sure to continue – this is a young family and enterprise to be reckoned with.

HELLO...
IS IT TEA
YOU'RE
LOOKING FOR?

Wholemeal
SMALL = £ 1.75
LARGE = £ 2.75

great
taste

The Bakehouse
CRUSHED AVOCADO, HARISSA FRIED DUCK EGG & TOASTED PEARL BARLEY ON TOAST

The combination of zingy flavours and contrasting textures in this dish make it really enjoyable to eat, whether for brunch, lunch or a light supper. Harissa is a Moroccan spice paste and can be found in good supermarkets, delis or online. For the bread, we recommend our wholemeal Great Taste award winner, of course!

Preparation time: 15 minutes | Cooking time: 2 minutes | Serves 4

Ingredients

4 ripe avocados

Chilli flakes, to taste

Sea salt flakes, to taste

Cracked black pepper, to taste

4 thick slices of organic stoneground wholemeal bread

4 duck eggs

1 jar rose harissa

Good quality rapeseed oil

500g pearl barley

1 lime, zested and juiced

Rocket, to serve

Method

First, make the crushed avocado mix. Cut all the avocados in half, running your knife around the stone. Remove the stone and spoon the flesh into a mixing bowl. Add the lime zest and juice and season to taste with the chilli flakes, sea salt and pepper. Now crush the avocado using a fork and mix in the seasoning at the same time, to form a rustic but spreadable mix. Cover and set aside.

In another small bowl or mug, make the harissa dressing. Mix two parts rose harissa with one part rapeseed oil and add a little sea salt to taste. It's worth making a larger batch of this, as it's also amazing as a salad dressing or marinade.

Next, toast the pearl barley grains in a dry frying pan, stirring regularly over a low heat until golden brown and with a slight nutty flavour. The toasted grains can be kept until needed and will last to use with other dishes.

The key part of this dish is the frying of the duck egg. Follow the next instructions carefully to end up with a perfectly cooked white, with no burnt edges, and a rich runny yolk. The trick to a perfect fried egg is cooking it out slowly. Place your frying pan over a medium heat with a little oil. While the pan is warming up, place your sliced bread in the toaster and toast to your preference. When the pan and oil are warm, crack in the eggs. Use a spatula to help the egg keep its shape and don't allow it to spread to much while the white sets. The egg should cook slowly without spitting and bubbling. To season simply add a little sea salt to the yolk when it's nearly ready.

To serve

While the egg is slowly cooking, layer a handful of rocket on each of the four plates. The toast should be ready, so spread each slice with a thick layer of the avocado mix and place on top of the rocket. When the whites are set and the yolks are still runny, place an egg on top of each slice of avocado-topped toast and spoon over the harissa dressing (about one tablespoon per dish). To finish the dish, sprinkle over the toasted pearl barley and serve.

The Bakehouse
SALAD OF COLSTON BASSETT STILTON, HOMEMADE PICKLES AND WALNUTS

When pulling this dish together, it really is up to you how much of each component you want on the plate. The real satisfaction comes from making your own pickles. Like baking, pickling is a real artisan skill and one that, once mastered, can be tweaked and experimented with.

Preparation time: 10 minutes, plus 1-2 weeks pickling time | Serves 4

Ingredients

Colston Bassett Stilton (as much or little as you like)

Pickled beetroot (see method)

Sweet pickled pear (see method)

Walnut halves, toasted

Good quality salted butter

Wholemeal, rye or multi-seed bread

Sea salt flakes

2 litres white wine vinegar

4 bay leaves

2 tbsp coriander seed

2 tbsp fennel seeds

1 tbsp chilli flakes

300g caster sugar

200g table salt

Mixed leaves

Method

To make the pickles, first cook the beetroot. We recommend roasting the beetroot wrapped in foil with salt, pepper and a little oil for around an hour at 180°c, depending on the size of the beetroot. Peel the beetroot whilst it's still warm, and cut into wedges. Place the wedges into a sterilised jar and set aside.

Now cut the pears lengthways into thin slices and place these into a separate sterilised jar along with two teaspoons of sugar.

To make the pickling liquid, set a saucepan large enough to hold 2.5 litres of water over a medium heat. Both of the pickles in this dish use the same pickling liquid, with a little more sugar added to the pears. Lightly toast the coriander and fennel seeds in the saucepan, and then add the bay leaves and chilli flakes to release all the flavours. Add the vinegar, salt and sugar and bring to the boil. Remove from the heat and allow to cool slightly. Pour the liquid over the beetroot and the pears until they're completely covered, and seal the jars. The pickling process happens fairly quickly but for optimum flavour it's worth leaving them for 1-2 weeks before you use them.

For the final dish, you'll also need to toast the walnut halves in a dry frying pan on a low heat until they start to colour. Combine your homemade pickles, toasted walnuts with generous lumps of Stilton and a handful of mixed leaves. Serve with sliced bread and butter. Simple, but very tasty!

Share and
SHARE ALIKE

Bar Iberico is an all-day tapas bar and the easy going sister of Iberico World Tapas in Nottingham, boasting its own fantastic menu, drinks selection and beautifully designed seating areas for everyone to kick back and relax with great sharing food from breakfast to supper.

Owners Dan Lindsay and Jacque Ferreira had a vision for a more relaxed, accessible, simplified dining experience that embraced the key elements of their successful Iberico World Tapas Nottingham and Derby restaurants. The result was an all-day tapas bar, designed with social interaction and flexibility in mind, where the buzzy yet easy going vibes have drawn literally thousands of customers to its door every week since the opening in August 2016.

The menu embraces both classic Spanish flavours and the concept of sharing, which allows and encourages customers to sample a varied selection of dishes in a group. Crispy Chicken with Spicy Jerez Sauce, and the Portuguese Custard Tarts made in-house twice daily may be highlights, but there is plenty to choose from, organised into sections including breakfast, charcuterie and cheese, pinchos (skewers) which are cooked using the charcoal-fuelled Josper Grill, and topped flatbreads made fresh to order in the wood-fired oven. Executive head chef Jacque designs the regularly updated menu around seasonal produce which the team source locally where possible, accompanied by the best authentic ingredients from Spanish suppliers. This is complemented by informed and welcoming front-of-house service, overseen by general manager Richard Ford.

The clientele are generally as diverse as the food, and with no reservations everybody from freelancers to families can drop by and feel completely at ease. Many customers say they feel like they're in Spain itself at Bar Iberico, and credit must go not only to Dan but also to his mum Jan, as they designed the restaurant interior together. The ground floor is light and airy, with a central bar from which tables radiate outwards, offering a view of the open kitchen. The downstairs seating area has its own quirks and adds an intimate feel – it can also be booked out for private parties. The Mediterranean ambiance is also enhanced by an al fresco dining area, on sunny days at least!

Bar Iberico's popularity and its runaway success as a city centre destination has led Dan and Jacque to think about opening up more branches of the all-day tapas hotspot in other cities in the very near future. Fans and newcomers alike watch this space – we expect that the Iberico team will continue bringing the sunshine of the Med to Nottingham and elsewhere with their signature style and flavour!

Bar Iberico

Photo: Darren Ciolli-Leach

Bar Iberico
OCTOPUS, CONFIT POTATO, SMOKED PAPRIKA

This is a classic Spanish favourite, and is deceptively simple to prepare. We use 2-3kg double sucker octopus at the restaurant. They are caught in the Mediterranean Sea and then block frozen; the freezing and thawing helps tenderise the meat.

Preparation time: 15 minutes | Cooking time: approximately 1½ hours | Serves 4

Ingredients

1 thawed double sucker octopus (approximately 2-3 kg)

1 carrot, chopped

1 onion, chopped

2 sticks celery, chopped

1 garlic bulb, halved

2 sprigs of thyme

2 bay leaves

500g new potatoes

500ml good-quality olive oil

½ tsp smoked paprika

1 tsp chopped parsley

Maldon sea salt, to taste

1 lemon

1 tsp capers

Method

Place the octopus in an ovenproof dish with a lid, and add the chopped carrot, onion, celery, half the garlic, 1 sprig of thyme and 1 bay leaf. Drizzle everything with a couple of tablespoons of olive oil and season with Maldon sea salt. Cover with the lid and cook for 1½ hours at 150°c.

While the octopus is cooking, prepare the potatoes. Place the new potatoes in a saucepan with the remaining garlic, bay leaf and thyme. Cover with olive oil and place on a medium heat until the oil reaches 90°c. Turn down the heat and keep the olive oil around 90°c for about an hour, or until the potatoes are just tender.

To serve

When the octopus and potatoes are tender, slice everything up into 1cm thick rounds. Arrange the rounds on a plate, then sprinkle over a few pinches of smoked paprika, Maldon sea salt, capers and parsley and add a squeeze of fresh lemon juice.

Finally, drizzle a tablespoon of the olive oil over the dish and serve to impressed guests!

Black is the NEW BLACK

With a seasonally-inspired menu that's far from predictable, The Black Bull at Blidworth is pulling out all the stops to create delicious, flavour-driven cuisine in a cosy 18ᵗʰ century setting in rural Nottinghamshire.

Walking into The Black Bull at Blidworth, customers may well be in for a pleasant surprise if the traditional exterior, set against its small village backdrop, has led them to expect the usual pub fare. The building itself dates back to the early 1700s, and retains a warming dollop of character, but has been given a stylish makeover to bring the bar and restaurant, as well as the inviting B&B rooms above, bang up to date.

It's The Black Bull's menu that truly sets it apart though; nothing about the kitchen's ethos belongs to the past here. The outlook is wide-ranging, embracing cuisines from all over the world, and this is absolutely reflected in the mouth-watering and genuinely exciting dishes on offer – monkfish tikka or crab tartlet with summer truffle, anyone?

Head chefs Lewis Kuciers and Craig Hadden are both 21 years old, and yet they are the oldest members of the kitchen team. Rightly so, The Black Bull prides itself on this youthful talent – the restaurant had been awarded two rosettes by the time Lewis and Craig were just 20. They are ambitious, too, already pushing for that third rosette as well as aiming for a Michelin star in the future.

Lewis summarises the kitchen ethos as 'every dish better than the last' which is reason enough to visit in itself, but they also update the menu regularly to reflect the best local produce available – if grouse comes into season on 12th August, they'll have it on the menu by the 15th. Regulars at The Black Bull seem to know a good thing when they eat at one; customers return as frequently as every few weeks, eager to sample the latest addition to the constantly evolving menu. Some even bring their own contributions; free beer in return for fresh eggs is not unheard of amongst the savvier locals.

Though you might have come across more than one Black Bull in the English countryside, this particular freehouse is something special – with such promise so early on, it's not to be missed.

The Black Bull at Blidworth
WAGYU BEEF WITH RAW BEEF TACO AND BURNT HOTDOG ONIONS

When the chefs at The Black Bull create this dish, the beef they use is sourced from Earl Stonham Farm in Suffolk, home of the only commercial pure-bred wagyu herd in the UK. Wagyu refers to any of the four Japanese breeds of beef cattle, which have an incredibly high level of fat marbling, resulting in very rich, juicy, melt-in-the-mouth steak.

Preparation time: 36 hours approximately | Cooking time: 14 hours | Serves 4

Ingredients

For the beef:

1kg wagyu beef brisket

1 litre water

10g peppercorns

50g fresh tarragon

10g star anise

200g Maldon sea salt

1 litre dark ale

2 litres beef stock

For the tacos:

200g plain flour

Pinch of salt

Water

For the raw beef mix:

200g chives

300ml vegetable oil

3 egg yolks

Lemon juice, to taste

100ml white wine vinegar

80g sugar

2 shallots

100g wagyu bavette

30g capers

For the garnishes:

1kg banana shallots, peeled and sliced

125g unsalted butter

½ pint of ale

2 large white onions

250g butter

8 banana shallots, thinly sliced

3 Roscoff onions, peeled and halved

4 potatoes, peeled

Handful of panko breadcrumbs

Method

Trim off any excess fat from the wagyu brisket and set aside, keeping the fat. To make the brine, bring the water to a boil, add the peppercorns, tarragon and star anise, then whisk in the salt until it's fully dissolved. Add the beer and place the brine in the fridge for about 3 hours, or until cold. Submerge the piece of beef in the brine and place back in the fridge for 24 hours.

Preheat the oven to 110°c. Remove the beef from the brine, wash thoroughly and pat dry. Place the beef into a large cassoulet dish and submerge it in the beef stock. Cook in the oven for about 8 hours, or until soft. Place the beef on a baking tray lined with cling film, cover it with cling film, then put another baking sheet on top of the beef with around 5kg of weight on top of that. Leave this in the fridge for at least 8 hours to press, then remove from the fridge and cut the beef into four cubes.

To make the tacos, place the flour and salt in a bowl and add water to form a tacky dough. Leave this to rest for 20 minutes. For the chive mayonnaise, blend the chives with the vegetable oil then pass through a fine sieve. Whisk the egg yolks and lemon juice together in a small bowl and slowly add the chive oil, whisking constantly to avoid the mixture splitting. Keep whisking until a mayonnaise-like texture forms and season to taste. Warm the white wine vinegar, dissolve the sugar in it and add the thinly sliced shallots. Next, dice the bavette and mix the pieces with the chive mayonnaise, capers and drained pickled shallots. Place this into the fridge for later.

Roll out the taco dough on a floured surface to about a 2mm thickness, and cut out circles with a three-inch round cutter. Cover and place into the fridge for later.

To make the three garnishes, first sweat the banana shallots in butter for about 2 hours. When they are soft, add the beer and reduce whilst allowing the shallots to caramelise slightly. Blend the mixture to form a smooth purée and set aside.

To make the onion ash, roast the two white onions at 200°c until they are fully blackened and dried. Blitz in a blender until powder, season the onions, pass through a sieve and set aside. Next, fry the sliced shallots in melted butter until they are golden and crispy, and leave to drain. To make the onion 'petals', place the Roscoff onions flat side down in a hot dry pan, leave to cool then carefully remove individual layers.

Now put the saved wagyu fat in the oven at 160°c for about an hour. Pour the rendered fat into a small saucepan, add the potatoes and cook on a low heat in a saucepan until soft. Fry the panko breadcrumbs in the leftover wagyu fat until golden brown, then drain.

To serve

Roast the cubes of wagyu beef in the oven for 12 minutes at 180°c. Preheat a dry frying pan and add the taco rounds one at a time. Cook for 10 seconds on each side then fill with the raw beef mixture. Add the onion petals into the fat with the potatoes for about a minute to warm through. Take the potatoes out, coat them in breadcrumbs and place onto the plate. Warm the shallot purée and spoon onto the plate. Place an onion petal on top of the purée, fill it with crispy shallots and season with the onion ash. Add the roasted beef and a beef taco to the plate to finish the dish.

Too Gouda
TO BE TRUE

Serious about coffee, but without expecting their customers to be,
Blend is creating a space for everyone to enjoy meeting, eating and drinking
in a relaxed atmosphere. Taking full advantage of an up-and-coming location in
Nottingham they're bringing the community together through great coffee
and grilled cheese sandwiches.

Blend was established in February 2017 with the intention of providing a shop window, so to speak, for Stewarts of Trent Bridge to showcase their artisan coffee. Stewarts was founded by a charismatic local businessman, Stewart Falconer, who purchased a 1978 German-made coffee roaster and brewed up Nottingham's first taste of hand roasted coffee in the mid-1980s.

He must have got his money's worth, because the original machine is still essential to Stewarts' coffee roasting process today and can be seen in action by interested café customers, who are invited to pop next door and take a tour of the roastery after finishing their not-so-regular cup of joe. You'd be hard pressed to find a fresher one, or one created with more care – co-directors Mark Whittaker, Nathan Barton and Monika Häfeli Barton are absolutely committed to giving people top quality coffee in every bag or cup they sell.

The café itself is a light, airy space designed to welcome all and sundry – an antithesis to those places that seem to cater for coffee connoisseurs only. General manager and head chef Danielle Von Suskil has created a menu inspired by her roots in New Jersey, full of grilled cheese sandwiches and other irresistible treats with names like 'Brieyonce' and 'The Kevin Baconator' – no prizes for guessing the secret ingredients in those two. There are vegan, dairy-free and gluten-free options aplenty though, and the menu changes seasonally, in keeping with the inclusive and down-to-earth ethos of the business.

Community spirit is very important to Blend, especially given that it has taken up residence in Sneinton Market, during the formerly unloved area's renovation and transformation into a thriving cultural and artistic hub for the city. Much of the café's produce makes a journey of mere minutes to reach the kitchen from Stonebridge City Farm, a volunteer-run charity and urban green space. Blend also makes use of the many local breweries on offer to complement the popcorn and snacks they serve at their popular outdoor cinema events.

Whether you're a carnivore, herbivore or 'dessertivore' as the café menu has it, the combination of café and roastery is turning out to be a perfect blend of intentions and passions – coffee and grilled cheese sandwiches made with love and served with a smile.

Blend

DRINKS
ESPRESSO
AMERICANO
LATTE
CAPPUCCINO
FLAT WHITE
Coffee

BLEND

Blend
DREW BERRYMORE GRILLED CHEESE DESSERT SANDWICH

A fun and indulgent recipe for pun and cheese lovers alike, this sandwich is ideal for breakfast, lunch, dinner or indeed dessert, according to chef Dani. You could experiment with lots of different cheeses for the filling – as long as they are good melting cheeses the result will be just as oozy and delicious as the recommended combo!

Preparation time: 5-10 minutes | Cooking time: 8 minutes | Serves 1

Ingredients

2 slices sourdough

Butter or margarine

25g soft rindless goat's cheese

25g mascarpone cheese

120g grated cheese (we use a combination of Cheddar, Emmental and mozzarella)

35g white chocolate chips

3-4 fresh strawberries, sliced, plus 1 whole one for garnish

Icing sugar, to garnish

Method

Liberally butter the outside of each slice of bread with margarine or unsalted butter. Carefully place each slice, butter side down, onto baking paper to prevent the sandwich from sticking to the work surface whilst assembling.

Combine the goat's cheese and mascarpone until evenly blended, then spread the cheese mixture over one slice of bread. Layer the grated cheese evenly onto the other slice of bread. Sprinkle the white chocolate over the grated cheese, and place the strawberries on the other slice, pressing them into the soft cheese to stick them into place.

Carefully press both halves together to assemble the sandwich. Apply light pressure to make sure all the fillings are stuck into place.

We use a griddle and irons to cook our sandwiches; however two frying pans would do the trick!

Preheat the griddle or frying pan to a medium heat. Place the sandwich on it; there should be a sizzle. Place an iron or a second preheated frying pan on top of the sandwich to start cooking the topside and hold everything together. Leave to cook for 3-4 minutes until golden brown.

Carefully flip the sandwich, and repeat the process for another 3-4 minutes until golden brown on both sides.

Remove it from the griddle and slice in half. If the cheese is not completely melted, return to the heat for a few minutes until the filling is nice and oozy.

To serve

Garnish with a dusting of icing sugar and fresh strawberries, and tuck in immediately!

Spreading
HAPPINESS

Transforming blue-sky thinking to blue-sky drinking, the quirky, independent Bluebird Tea Co. is a dynamic young business with creativity at its heart. Bluebird's mixology team follow the mission statement to put a smile into each and every day with their original Wall of Tea.

November marked a happy month for Nottingham, as the independent and innovative Bluebird Tea Co. opened their brand new shop at No.5 Victoria Street, bringing original tea blends and blue sky days back to the city. Although Bluebird Tea Co. has spent the last few years at its 'Nest' in Brighton, the business was actually born in Nottingham. Co-owner and founder Krisi grew up in Nuthall and is very happy to be returning to her hometown for 2017, having grown her company to become one of the country's leading tea innovators.

From their roots as Bluebird, the mixologists are moving into 2018 with new branding that will continue to communicate the innovative, friendly and fun ethos of the company. The original name was inspired by the term 'bluebird day' when owners Krisi and Mike were living in Canada, which denotes a perfect day with bright blue skies: the type of day where people smile and feel like anything is possible. On their return to the UK in 2013, Krisi's mum gave the couple a six month grace period and the use of her back bedroom, from which they packed tea to sell at markets across Nottingham every weekend.

During this time, the company gained a loyal following of customers who were passionate about their products – many of these same people still buy Bluebird tea online.

The continual process of developing new tea blends is Krisi's favourite part of her job; four years and over 100 types of tea later, Krisi still does this by hand for every new blend. Just one look at the shelves makes it clear that fun and flavour come first: these are teas to make you smile. New flavours inspired by the seasons are created all the time – think Strawberry Lemonade in summer (lovely served chilled) or Gingerbread Chai in the winter. Teas can be ordered from the website or bought in the shop, where expert tea mixologists are on hand to dispense advice and guidance so you can find your perfect blend.

Bluebird Tea Co. is thrilled with the location of its brand new Nottingham shop just off the Old Market Square, with its beautiful big windows and the lovely architectural details picked out in blue paint. It's also surrounded by many of Nottingham's amazing independent food and drink businesses such as 200 Degrees Coffee Roasters and Homemade, in the great company of both Hockley and Main Street custom. Krisi and Mike are proud to now ship to an impressive 65 countries and have 280 shareholders, all of whom are customers and fans of their award-winning teas. Bluebird Tea Co. continues to spread its wings across the UK into 2018, sharing happiness with every cup.

Bluebird Tea Co.

JASMINE POACHED PEARS
Jasmine green tea lightly scented with fruity pear

LEMONADE
When life gives you lemons, brew lemonade.

BLUE RASPBERRY
Watch this beautiful Blue blend change colour before your

PURE GRADE MATCHA

Have a Bluebird Day...

Welcome to Bluebird Tea Co.!
We are the UK's expert Tea Mixologists on a
mission to spread happiness one cup at a time.

We are a local, independent business who,
in just a few short years, have grown from
packing tea in our bedroom to Brighton's
sunny south coast. We create all of our blend
recipes + hand pack them in our little
warehouse in Hove.

The name comes from the skiing term meaning
with blue skies and fresh snow.
When everything is beautiful +
possible. It is flying. It is freedom.

COLD BREW TEA
BLUEBIRD TEA CO.
Fruit Salad

COLD BREW TEA
BLUEBIRD TEA CO.
Pandalicious Liquorice

COLD BREW TEA
BLUEBIRD TEA CO.
Fruit Salad

INGERBREAD

CHAI

great taste

'ward-winning spiced gingerbread
chai'

BLUEBIRD TEA CO.
IXOLOGISTS

Bluebird Tea Co.
ALL THINGS SPICED
GINGERBREAD CHAI LATTE

Our bestselling tea latte, made with real spices and fresh, sweet milk –
Gingerbread Chai is a hug in a mug! Try our tea twist to turn this fab latte into
an iced and spiced rum cocktail too!

Preparation time: 10 minutes | Serves 1

Ingredients

*1 tsp or 2 bags Bluebird Tea Co.
Gingerbread Chai Tea*

1 tsp honey

Sprinkle of cinnamon

Sprinkle of nutmeg

Milk

Dark rum (optional)

Ice (optional)

Method

Brew two teaspoons of tea (or two tea bags) in 100ml of hot water for at least four minutes. Add 1 teaspoon of honey and then 200ml of hot frothed milk – use a handheld frother or an aerator machine. Pour into your favourite mug and sprinkle with cinnamon or nutmeg.

For a naughty alternative add a shot of dark rum and some ice to turn this into a luxurious cocktail – you know you want to!

Enjoy!

Not just the
DAILY GRIND

Cartwheel roasts its own coffee and cooks everything on the food menu from scratch, making the café on Nottingham's upmarket Low Pavement a destination with something for everyone.

Cartwheel Café and Roastery opened in June 2016 and is already thriving on the basis of owner Alex Bitsios-Esposito's belief that amazing food and amazing coffee don't have to be mutually exclusive. Winners of the 2017 Best Café award from Nottinghamshire Food and Drink, Cartwheel focuses on healthy, modern brunch dishes and of course great coffee any way you want it. Options including pour-overs, siphons, single origin brews, tasting flights and even tea made with the coffee cherry make the drinks menu extensive, exciting and fit for a coffee-lovers paradise.

Head chef Lee Simpson has a background in fine dining, so there's no scrimping on quality across the food menu, whether you're ordering a pancake stack to enjoy with friends, or picking up a sandwich for lunch on the hoof. There's a lovely selection of brunch dishes which are almost build-your-own: eggs are the key component to which you can add bacon; smashed avocado; homemade baked beans; new potato hash; smoked salmon and more – all served on sourdough from the lovely Welbeck Bakehouse. Seasonal specials are updated every month, such as current favourite autumnal pumpkin pie, made with pumpkins from Lee's mum's allotment!

Alex has made sure that Cartwheel is very Nottingham-centric when it comes to suppliers, except of course for the coffee beans, which the roastery buys green after tasting as many as 50 varieties from the area (which could be in Kenya, Colombia, or Ethiopia – it all depends on the best harvests) before deciding which to purchase. If customers can't get enough of the drinks made at the café, they can buy bags of the same beans, prepared at the Cartwheel Roastery, to take home and enjoy. The café also prides itself on its provision for those with special dietary requirements, and the team know exactly what's in each dish as everything is made there from scratch.

Opening a café and roastery has been a long-standing goal for Alex, having grown up helping in his mum's coffee shop in Beeston and gone on to train as a barista and coffee roaster before setting up Cartwheel as an embodiment of everything he's passionate about when it comes to coffee, food, hospitality and ambience – a perfect storm that you won't want to pass over!

Cartwheel Café

LIME AND CORIANDER CURED SALMON WITH AVOCADO, WILTED SPINACH AND POACHED EGG ON SOURDOUGH

This lovely dish combines zingy flavour from the lime and coriander cure with the sweetness of salmon and the mild taste of spinach and avocado. The poached eggs should have runny yolks, to create a kind of sauce for the dish – swirling the water before adding the eggs helps them keep their shape and cook evenly.

Preparation time: 15 minutes, plus 2-3 hours curing | Cooking time: 10 minutes | Serves 2

Ingredients

200g table salt

200g caster sugar

1 lime, zested and juiced

40g fresh coriander

10g toasted coriander seeds

2 x 100g salmon fillets, skinned and boned

1 large ripe avocado

A pinch of Maldon sea salt

A pinch of black pepper

4 tbsp white wine vinegar

1 tbsp vegetable oil

Handful of pumpkin seeds and linseeds, toasted

20g butter

200g baby leaf spinach, washed

2 free-range eggs

A drizzle of olive oil

2 thick slices of sourdough, toasted

Method

Place the salt, sugar, lime zest, coriander and seeds in a food processor and blend until the ingredients are combined. Place half of the mix in a container, lay the salmon on top and cover the fillets with the remaining cure. After 2-3 hours in the fridge rinse under cold water and place on a cloth to dry.

Next, cut the avocado in half and scrape the flesh into a bowl using a spoon. Smash the avocado using a fork, and season with the Maldon salt, black pepper and lime juice. Cover and set aside.

Pour water into a medium-sized saucepan until it's three quarters full, add the vinegar and bring the water to a simmer. Heat the vegetable oil in a non-stick frying pan, and cook the salmon over a medium heat for about 1 minute on each side. Take the salmon out of the pan, place it on a cloth and sprinkle over the toasted seeds.

Now add the butter to the pan and wilt the spinach. While the spinach is wilting, stir the pan of simmering water until a slight well forms in the centre. Crack both eggs into this well and poach for 4 minutes. Remove the eggs from the water with a slotted spoon, drain on a cloth and season with salt and pepper.

To serve

Drizzle the olive oil over the toasted sourdough and spread the wilted spinach over both slices. Place the salmon fillets on top of the spinach. Using a spoon, gently lift the eggs and place them to one side of the toasts. Scoop the smashed avocado onto the centre of the plate and serve straightaway.

More cheese, PLEASE!

The Cheese Shop Nottingham is 15 years young, now includes a licensed café, and brothers Rob and Webb Freckingham are as much a fixture of the food scene here as ever.

Five years ago The Cheese Shop Nottingham moved to its current, larger premises, and demand is so constant that although owners Rob and Webb like to play things by ear, they certainly wouldn't turn down the opportunity to take on another shop in the future. You couldn't meet a more down-to-earth pair, despite successes including Nottinghamshire Food and Drink Café of the Year and an Observer Food Monthly award. Though they do occasionally get recognised and offered a pint or two by locals, they are modest about their achievements and are simply not in it for the awards.

For Webb, the customers and the variety of his work days are the real draw, though cheese through the post seems like an excellent perk too – as the shop's reputation has grown – Rob and Webb often receive parcels of artisan cheese from makers wanting to be stocked there! No wonder they are popular in their local, as Friday nights often become unofficial 'taste testing' sessions for patrons.

The Cheese Shop has cultivated a real connection with its suppliers, as well as its customers, and both brothers now travel around the country regularly to collect from the smaller producers whose cheese they stock in person. Big names include Barkham Blue, Montgomery Cheddar and Charles Martell, and of course Stilton from local heroes Colston Bassett Dairy and Cropwell Bishop Creameries. They stick to a simple rule when stocking their shop and café – they don't sell anything they wouldn't eat themselves.

The café is an excellent spot to enjoy all this fantastic artisan cheese from the UK as well as overseas, as well as some tasty local products, including pork pies from Mrs King's Pies. The café is licenced, so customers can enjoy a good Port or the popular choice of Sauterns (a dessert wine) with their cheeseboard, sandwich or scone which are fresh every morning. Rob and Webb are adamant that when it comes to pairings, there are no hard and fast rules, and it's a matter of individual taste. There certainly is a taste for such an accommodating and knowledgeable pair in Nottingham – long may their dedication to serving and selling the very best cheeses continue.

The Cheese Shop
FARMER'S FONDUE

Fondue was originally a Swiss invention, designed to use up old cheese and stale bread, but since being welcomed with open arms by the rest of the world it has garnered more of a romantic, and certainly an indulgent, reputation. Webb gives specific portion sizes for this fondue, which feeds four but only if they're not greedy, which we wouldn't count on when this fondue's in front of them…

Preparation time: 10 minutes | Cooking time: 10 minutes | Serves 4 … or 2 greedy ones!

Ingredients

180g Montgomery's cheddar

100g Ogleshield cheese

200ml beer (we use Shipstones, a local beer)

1 garlic clove

2 tbsp cornflour

2 tsp powered English mustard

White pepper, to taste

For dipping:

Cubes of crusty bread

Cherry tomatoes

Cooked cocktail sausages

Celery or carrot batons

Picked onions

Cornichons

Caper berries

Apple slices

Method

Slice the garlic clove in half and rub the inside of the pot all over with the cut side. Pour in the beer, and heat gently on the hob.

Grate both cheeses into a bowl, add the corn flour and mustard and mix well. When the beer is hot, slowly add the cheese mixture a handful at a time, until the cheese has melted. Stir the mixture with a wooden spoon and repeat the process until the cheese has all been incorporated.

When all the cheese is melted and the fondue is smooth, season with pepper to taste. If the fondue is a little thick, add a drop more beer or boiled water to thin it down.

To serve

Decant the fondue into a fondue set and in Rob's and Webb's words, get dipping!

A trip
THROUGH TIME

Rebecca White runs The Clock House café and tea room at Upton Hall, serving home baked scones, cakes, breakfasts and wholesome meals since 2013 in a venue decked out in traditional style, complete with tastefully mismatched furniture and vintage china.

It's not every day that you find a café and tea room in the home of the British Horological Institute. Upton Hall provides the perfect venue for the old-timey charm of The Clock House, where it's easy to while away an afternoon tucking into the legendary scones whose flavours change according to the season (think autumnal cinnamon with Bramley apple compote), accompanied by one of the many loose leaf teas available, all served in proper teapots, of course.

The menu doesn't stray far from what you'd expect from tasty tea room fare, including homemade cakes, light meals, and breakfasts served all day – but it's the quality of the food and the emphasis on exceptional service that set The Clock House apart. The produce used for the breakfasts is so good customers often end up ordering second helpings – the bacon comes from GH Porter, and the sausages are provided by Richards, both traditional butchers based in nearby Newark.

Staff at The Clock House pride themselves on the delicious food, and also on the welcome they give each and every customer, whether a local regular, a new visitor or one of the many international students who pop in on a break from training at the BHI. Rebecca White has led the team since taking on the business in January 2016, with Helen Bett – manager and consultant for all the gluten-free menu options, being a coeliac herself – and Jodie Coombes – a relatively new but invaluable addition to the kitchen – right by her side. The talented trio also provide catering for events at The Clock House, as the space is available for private hire right into the evenings, though afternoon tea parties have proved a popular choice at the relaxed, intimate venue.

Rebecca herself has, in her own words, 'always cooked' – she made her name locally cooking in pubs including The French Horn and the Waggon and Horses, and moved onto the café scene after her children were born. Always looking for ways to evolve and consolidate her passion for being in the kitchen, Rebecca now caters for groups at the Horspool Luxury Retreat, and is also a private chef, under the business name Rebecca White Cooks.

The Clock House is clearly thriving with such an experienced owner and committed team, and continues to build on its successes, providing a unique dining experience for everyone who books an event there or happens on the peaceful setting with its friendly, and tasty, welcome.

The Clock House

Breakfast omelette with sausage, mushroom + tomato £6.80 add bacon £7.50

Smoked salmon + sc...

Avocado + goat's cheese on toast £6.90

Warm croissant filled with ham + cheese £4.20 or mushroom + brie £4.20

The Clock House
EGGS BENEDICT

Eggs Benedict has to be the ultimate decadent brunch. The origins of this dish date back to 1890's New York, and it's believed that it was created at the Waldorf as a hangover cure for retired Wall Street stockbroker Lemuel Benedict. Done well, it's fit for a king, never mind a stockbroker!

Preparation time: 10 minutes | Cooking time: 20 minutes| Serves 4

Ingredients

For the vinegar reduction:

200ml white wine vinegar

100ml dry white wine

1 shallot, roughly chopped

6 peppercorns, crushed

10 parsley stalks

1 bay leaf

For the muffins:

4 English muffins, sliced

250g unsalted butter, softened

8 slices baked thick-carved ham

For the hollandaise:

3 egg yolks

2 tbsp white wine vinegar

Salt, to taste

½ lemon, juiced

For the poached eggs:

8 free-range eggs

Method

Start by placing all the ingredients for the vinegar reduction into a saucepan and bringing the mixture to the boil. Reduce by half, strain and leave to cool. This can be kept in a sealed container in the fridge for 3 months.

Toast all the muffins and butter lightly, then lay a slice of ham on each muffin half and set aside on a baking tray ready for reheating. Preheat the oven to 160°c and bring a large pan of water with the white wine vinegar into just below simmering point (about 95°c).

Next, melt the remaining butter until it bubbles. In a glass bowl that sits snugly over the pan of simmering water, whisk three egg yolks, two tablespoons of the vinegar reduction and two tablespoons of water together. Keep whisking quite vigorously over the simmering water until the egg yolks start to increase in volume. Once the mixture has at least doubled in volume, start drizzling the warm butter in, a little at a time so it emulsifies like a mayonnaise as it's whisked. When a third of the butter has been incorporated, take the bowl off the heat and add the remaining butter (leaving the watery residue at the bottom) slowly whilst still whisking. The hollandaise should be the thickness of ¾ whipped double cream and leave ribbon patterns on the surface of the mixture when the whisk is lifted out. If the hollandaise thickens too much, add a teaspoon of water to loosen it.

Season the sauce to taste with salt and lemon juice and keep it warm. Place the tray with the assembled muffin halves, along with four plates, into the warm oven for 2-3 minutes. Crack your 8 eggs into individual ramekins or bowls, gently stir the simmering water in the pan the sauce was cooked over to create a whirlpool motion and slide the eggs in one at a time. Poach each egg for around two minutes, until the white is set and the yolk is cooked but still runny inside.

To serve

Take the warmed muffins out of the oven and place two halves on each of the four warmed plates. Remove the poached eggs from the pan with a slotted spoon and drain. Place an egg on each ham-topped muffin half, then spoon over the rich hollandaise.

A perfect start to any day!

Heart and SOLE

Whether you choose to eat in the relaxed restaurant, pick up a takeaway for that Friday night treat, or take home the daily catch from the fishmonger's counter, The Cod's Scallops is the place to go for all your fish and chip or seafood needs.

John Molnar opened The Cod's Scallops Wollaton in 2011 with the aim of creating a 'hybrid' fish and chip shop, where customers could eat in or takeaway knowing that the seafood they bought was as fresh as possible and top quality. The Cod's Scallops Sherwood followed in the spring of 2016, keeping to the same model, and John's thriving business placed third at the National Fish & Chip Awards that same year, having already scooped Best Newcomer in 2014. The drive behind such success comes down to John's ethos when it comes to fish and seafood – it's about quality not quantity, keeping it simple, and showcasing the best of what's landed in Britain every day.

The Cod's Scallops works with great suppliers up and down the UK coast, including Nottingham Seafood, to bring in the freshest daily catch for the wet fish counter as well as the takeaway and eat-in menus. This means that, rather than just the usual suspects, the chefs and fishmongers can work with up to twenty different types of fish and seafood on any given day. Those that aren't available there and then are listed as 'Still at Sea' and menu prices sometimes alter according to market variations – it's important to John and the team as a whole that emphasis is on what's best and in season, not just what's in demand.

Both the eat-in and takeaway menus are extensive, and full of firm favourites as well as lesser known options. The food is cooked to order by the team, many of whom are trained chefs including John himself, a chef by trade, who usually pitches in on 'Frydays' when everyone's keen to get their weekly fish and chip fix! However, as well as the traditional offerings there are delicious salads, baked rather than fried fish fillets, and a specials menu featuring irresistible fish soups and pies as the colder months set in, plus drinks and desserts to round the whole experience off. So even if you don't fancy anything battered in traditional beef dripping, you're still spoilt for choice whether eating in, taking away, or buying fresh fillets and seafood with expert advice on how to cook them at home from the wet fish counter.

The seaside-y feel of the venues reminds customers that it's all about celebrating the best of the British coast – staff sport knotted hankies and t-shirts with slogans such as 'Living the Bream' and the colourful décor is reminiscent of idyllic childhood holidays by the sea. It's a unique set-up, not least for a county as land-locked as Nottinghamshire, but John and the carefully selected team of local hospitality professionals have worked hard to create their success. The Cod's Scallops has just been shortlisted in the Top 20 for Independent Restaurant Fish and Chip Shop of the Year at the 2018 National Fish & Chip Awards, and with a third venue opening very soon at Long Eaton, it looks set to continue making waves when it comes to fantastic fish and chips!

The Cod's Scallops
GRILLED CORNISH MACKEREL, ROASTED BEETS, FETA, SPINACH AND PINE NUTS

This recipe is simplicity at its best, with beautifully contrasting textures and flavours. Depending on availability, The Cod's Scallops chefs use golden and baby beetroot – the dish looks even more colourful and inviting with the bright varieties of beets on the plate.

Preparation time: 10 minutes | Cooking time: approx. 1 hour | Serves 2

Ingredients

2 whole mackerel (ask your fishmonger to fillet and v-bone them)

4 assorted beetroot

80g feta cheese, diced

1 bag of baby spinach, washed

Handful of toasted pine nuts

1 lemon

Cold-pressed rapeseed oil

Salt and pepper

Method

Wash the beetroot then bake until tender at 180°c for 45-50 minutes. Peel, slice or dice the beetroot and marinade in two tablespoons of the oil and the juice of half the lemon.

Dress the spinach with oil, salt, pepper and a squeeze of lemon.

Preheat the grill for 10 minutes on the hottest setting, and place the mackerel skin side up on a baking tray, season and brush with oil. Place the fish under the grill for 6 to 8 minutes, then squeeze the remaining lemon juice over when done.

To serve

Place the spinach, beetroot, pine nuts and feta on a plate, top with the grilled mackerel and drizzle lightly with rapeseed oil.

The home of traditional STILTON

One of only six dairies within the holy trinity of UK counties that qualify to make Stilton, Colston Bassett Dairy is still proudly producing the 'king of cheeses' in the beautiful Nottinghamshire countryside, over 100 years since its humble beginnings.

It was the village doctor, William Windley, who first suggested that local farmers set up a cheesemaking co-operative in the early 20th century. Today the milk is supplied from four local farms, all located within a 1½ mile radius of the dairy.

Incredibly, many of the original families who became part of that co-operative are still involved in the business, proving beyond a doubt that this enterprise has stood the test of time. At the dairy today, all the steps in the cheesemaking process are undertaken by hand – from mixing the milk in the cheese vats, cutting the curds, ladling, milling, salting and mixing, to filling the hoops (cheese moulds). It's labour intensive, but also an intuitive process, requiring a practiced eye and no shortage of real passion. Luckily, Colston Bassett is blessed with both of these in the form of their dairy manager Billy Kevan, who has overseen the creation of Colston Bassett's cheeses since 1999.

Stilton can only be produced in three counties within the UK: Nottinghamshire, Derbyshire and Leicestershire. The milk used must be pasteurised local milk, and the cheesemaking process is governed by a very strict code. All this trouble is taken in part due to Stilton's PDO status – that's Protected Designation of Origin – which protects and promotes quality foodstuffs so consumers know that the product they are buying has been made to a certain recipe. In other words, if the cheese you're buying is named Stilton, is has to be the real deal.

Unsurprisingly, demand for this very special product is still growing from cheese-lovers around the world, and though Colston Bassett often find that their busiest time is around Christmas, the cheese made at the dairy is so creamy, smooth and mellow that it's surprisingly versatile, and is certainly too good to be kept just for cheeseboards!

Whilst maintaining its proud heritage, the dairy is currently implementing a ten year investment programme to keep up with demand. It's a winning combination, evidenced by the astounding number of awards bestowed on Colston Bassett's cheese. This includes winning two Supreme Champion titles in 2014 – long may the success continue.

Blue Stilton

First Quality Traditional Stilton Cheese
Colston Bassett
AND DISTRICT DAIRY LIMITED
Blue Stilton®

Colston Bassett
Shropshire Blue

Photo: Culture Magazine

Colston Bassett Dairy
LOBSTER MAC 'N' CHEESE

A luxurious take on an American comfort food classic, this mac 'n' cheese is sure to deliver on taste as well as looks. If you prefer a slighter milder sauce, try Colston Basset's delicately sweet Shropshire Blue in place of their creamy, mellow Stilton. For a real flourish at a dinner party or special occasion, serve back in the shell as suggested by Jordan Sclare, who created this dish for Colston Bassett Dairy. Jordan has worked at Gordon Ramsay's 3 Michelin-starred restaurant and been head chef at Nobu, as well as executive head chef at Buddha Bar London and Chotto Matte.

Preparation time: 15-20 minutes, plus chilling time | Cooking time: approx. 30 minutes| Serves 2

Ingredients

For the sauce:

75g butter

55g plain flour

530ml milk

1 tbsp Dijon mustard

1 tbsp sea salt

Pinch of black pepper

150g Colston Bassett Stilton (or Shropshire Blue), crumbled

For the lobster:

1 x 600g lobster, whole in shell

100g macaroni, cooked

Pinch of sea salt

Handful of Colston Bassett Stilton (or Shropshire Blue), crumbled

A few coriander leaves, chopped

½ lemon, zested

Method

To make the sauce, melt the butter in a saucepan, then add the flour and whisk to combine. Heat the milk gently with the mustard, add salt and pepper. Gradually add the warmed milk to the flour and butter mixture, whisking continually until smooth. Stir in the crumbled Colston Bassett Shropshire Blue or Stilton until melted.

For the lobster, place in boiling water for 2 minutes. Then remove the claws and place these back into the water for a further 3 minutes. Meanwhile, chill the lobster tail and body.

Once the claws are cooked, chill them before removing the meat. Butterfly the lobster and discard the stomach and gills, reserving the tail meat. Dice the tail and claw meat into roughly 2cm pieces. Set this aside with the shell.

To put the dish together, reheat the sauce in a pan with the rest of the lobster meat, then reheat the pasta in boiling salted water for a few seconds. Drain the pasta and add to the sauce. Mix the two together until thoroughly heated through.

Spoon the mac n' cheese back into the lobster shell, top with the rest of the Colston Bassett cheese and grill until golden and bubbling on top.

To serve

Place the whole lobster onto a serving plate. Sprinkle over the finely chopped coriander and lemon zest – the residual heat will really bring out the aromatic flavours in the garnishes, and they will cut beautifully through the richness of the cheese sauce.

All the right ELEMENTS

Copper Cafés comprises three stylish venues in West Bridgford, Mapperley Top and Nottingham city centre, all of which serve breakfast right through to cocktails in luxurious surroundings.

The Copper brand is part of the independent company Great Northern Inns, which has stayed true to its name by opening high-quality pubs, bars and restaurants in and around the city of Nottingham. The company decided to venture into the café scene in 2009, with the opening of Copper West Bridgford. The second Copper venue in Mapperley arrived in 2014, and the city centre Copper was hot on its heels, opening in 2015. Each has links to the others through the sleek décor, the quality of the food and the morning to evening table service, but they all have their distinctive features suited to the area they can be found in.

Still one of the most popular spots for breakfast as well as a relaxed evening out in West Bridgford, the café, bar and lounge hosts live music every Sunday and has extra upstairs space, which is available for private hire and perfect for the more discerning public, with its plush seating and freelancer-friendly design. Outdoor seating offers an ideal spot for people-watching in warmer seasons, a feature which customers at Copper Mapperley can also enjoy. The Mapperley venue holds speciality evenings such as 'Steak Frites' and 'Moules' menus, catering for all tastes. The city centre Copper is the largest of the three and always busy – attracting passersby wanting a break from the crowds and theatre-goers from just across the road – offering pre-theatre set menus as well as a delicious brunch menu with bottomless cocktails every Sunday.

Each Copper serves a wide variety of food and drink right through the day, with coffee from Lee and Fletcher that's roasted in the city, and cakes from You Dessert It. The company as a whole is dedicated to supporting local businesses and people, so the staff all live nearby and provide friendly faces for the many regular customers. Some of these regulars visit every morning in the West Bridgford and Mapperley cafés, so it's lucky that Copper offers an extensive breakfast, lunch, afternoon tea and evening menu put together by a head chef at each location, with modern twists on traditionally tasty fare that it would be hard to get bored of.

Whether cravings for a cocktail, a full English breakfast or a tasty steak dinner hit you in Nottingham, Copper Cafés aim to provide the answer in stunning surroundings and a great atmosphere. What more could you ask of a city café, bar and lounge?

Copper Cafés
SAVOURY CHEESE SCONES WITH RED ONION MARMALADE

These scones are full of intense, savoury flavour – the sharpness of the mustard and cheese is complemented perfectly by the sweetness of the onion marmalade. Pomace oil, for cooking the red onion in, is a type of olive oil that can be bought in most supermarkets.

Preparation time: 20 minutes | Cooking time: approx. 45 minutes | Serves 6 (for two scones each)

Ingredients

For the cheese scones:

660g self-raising flour

215g margarine

2 level tbsp English mustard

2 level tbsp wholegrain mustard

15g baking powder

300g grated cheddar

Splash of milk

100g grated Parmesan

A little beaten egg to glaze

Salt and pepper, to season

For the red onion marmalade:

600g thinly sliced red onion

25g pomace oil

500ml red wine

50ml red wine vinegar

50g caster sugar

1 tsp salt

1 tsp black pepper

2 garlic cloves

2 bay leaves

10g picked thyme

Method

To make the scone mixture, put all the ingredients except for the milk, grated Parmesan and beaten egg in a mixing bowl and slowly mix. Once the margarine, cheese, mustards and flour are well combined, season well with salt and black pepper, then add enough milk just to bind the mixture into a firm dough. It shouldn't be too wet or sticky to roll out.

Turn the dough out onto a floured surface, and roll it out to around a 2 ½ cm thickness. Cut the dough into 6cm square scones and place on a greased and lined baking tray. They may look small, but they expand quite well so don't place them too close together.

Brush beaten egg over the top of all the scones and sprinkle over the grated Parmesan. Bake the scones at 180°c for 20 minutes, turning the trays after 12 minutes to ensure an even bake. When they are golden and well-risen, place the scones on a wire rack to cool while making the marmalade.

In a frying pan, slowly sweat the onions in the pomace oil without letting them colour. In a saucepan, reduce the wine and vinegar with the sugar, seasoning, garlic, bay and thyme in until only half the liquid remains. Strain the wine mixture through a sieve to remove any bits, and add the liquid to the onions. Reduce the marmalade to a desired stickiness; the more it reduces the more jam-like it becomes.

To serve

The head chef at Copper Cafés suggests splitting the cheese scones in half, spreading with cream cheese, and topping with a little (or a lot!) of the red onion marmalade.

Cakes and
CRAFTERNOONS

Debbie Bryan is a unique blend of creative experiences, beautiful handmade gifts, and delicious food and drink, located in Nottingham's historic Lace Market amongst the city's award-winning Creative Quarter.

The eponymous owner and founder of Debbie Bryan established her textile design studio in 2007 as a designer-maker, selling nationally and internationally. This evolving business keeps things fresh and interesting, responding to customers' feedback ensuring the company grows year on year. In 2009, this meant expanding their design studio to include a specialist retail space selling home textiles, handcrafted gifts, jewellery, ceramics, glassware and heritage pieces alongside the development of 'Crafternoons'. These can take the form of private bookable events and scheduled creative classes, from which the bi-annual creative feast SPEEDCraft (five Crafternoons in one day) originated; one of Debbie Bryan's most popular events.

Fast-forward to 2014 and Debbie Bryan introduced freshly baked cakes, seasonal lunches and a signature afternoon tea menu, made by Ashleigh, Robyn and Hannah, who alongside Katie, and Debbie herself, comprises the welcoming and creative team. Debbie Bryan also hosts pop-up evenings featuring chef Alex Bond from Alchemilla, the Rustic Crust and Poetry Nights with Big White Shed, and in 2016 they partnered with talented chef Craig Floate who delivers wonderful, diverse menus for his regular supperclubs.

The highly celebrated venue is a firm favourite for those looking for a great space and excellent service to host their own parties and events; perfect for those who want to try something a little different to the norm. The combination of a creative experience, friendly service, tasty food and drink,

unique gifts to purchase and the welcoming atmosphere at Debbie Bryan makes every visit special, and customers often remark that it's the perfect spot to relax and escape from the city centre hustle and bustle.

The shop and tea room is housed in a Georgian building, the interior of which is beautifully styled with lace heritage and textile nostalgia, and paired with a well-received music playlist. Debbie Bryan has cultivated a real connection with the region, not just through Nottingham's textile heritage and the collections made in-house, but through suppliers who provide the tea room with fantastic local produce. Freshly-roasted artisan coffee from Stewarts of Trent Bridge, and own brand real ales developed by Magpie Brewery go down nicely alongside Vork Pies which are a popular vegan fixture of the tea room menu, also featuring gluten-free bakes from Liberty Kitchen.

The accolades Debbie Bryan has earned over the years, highlighting the diversity of the venture and the love that goes into it, include Nottingham Creative Business Awards: Craft Winner, Nottinghamshire Stars Awards: Best New Venture, Nottingham Independent Business of the Year and Highly Commended in Food, Drink & Things to Do. In addition to the Lace Market venue, Debbie Bryan has two highly successful retail pop-ups, with ambitions to take these further afield, as well as continuing to develop and maintain all the much-loved aspects of this unique venture.

Debbie Bryan

Debbie Bryan
VEGAN CREAM TEA

This recipe was developed in collaboration with Debbie's mother-in-law Brenda Everett, originating from her own notes made when running their family bakery business. It wasn't a vegan recipe to begin with, but after much trial and error this recipe emerged and provides a delicious alternative to a traditional cream tea or a fantastic base to add sweet or savoury flavourings to – see our recommendations in the method below.

Preparation time: 20 minutes | Cooking time: approx. 10 minutes | Serves 12

Ingredients

For the scones:

450g self-raising flour

2 level tsp baking powder

Pinch of salt

85g caster sugar

170g vegan butter

200ml unsweetened almond milk

For the cream:

500ml coconut cream, chilled overnight

6 heaped tbsp icing sugar

Lemon juice, to taste

Method

Preheat the oven to 220°c and grease a baking tray with vegan butter. Add the flour, baking powder, salt and caster sugar into a mixing bowl and stir. Chop the vegan butter into small chunks and rub into dry ingredients using your fingertips.

These are our recommendations for sweet scones – choose your favourite, add to taste and mix well: Glacé cherry and desiccated coconut (wash and dry cherries before adding); sultana; date and walnut (finely chopped).

This recipe also works brilliantly for savoury and non-vegan scones. Our recommendations are: Pesto and fresh basil with fresh basil dressing; sun-dried tomato and sesame seed with sesame seed dressing; Stilton and walnut; feta and roasted red pepper; stem ginger and honey.

When any flavourings have been incorporated, add the unsweetened almond milk a little at a time and mix until you have soft pliable dough. Tip the scone dough onto a floured surface and knead very lightly, then roll out the dough to just over a centimetre thickness. Cut rounds from the dough and place them on the greased baking tray.

Brush the tops of all the scones with the remaining unsweetened almond milk, and bake in the preheated oven for 10-12 minutes until risen and golden brown. Allow to cool on the baking tray.

Whilst the scones are baking, make the whipped coconut and lemon cream. Take the coconut cream out of the fridge and add it to the icing sugar and a squeeze of lemon juice (approximately 2 teaspoons, or to taste) in a large mixing bowl. Beat until soft peaks form.

To serve

For sweet scones, dust with icing sugar and team with your favourite preserve. Serve with fresh strawberries on the side and a pot of tea to hand.

Word on
THE STREET

Edward's takes inspiration from all over the world for its eclectic menu of street food, served with a theatrical flourish that makes a visit to the award-winning Beeston restaurant a fine dining experience, not just a meal.

The eponymous owner of the unique street food restaurant that has enlivened Beeston since May 2015 has an irrepressible enthusiasm for his work. Edward Danby made the leap from telecoms to fine dining to start his new career, training in renowned restaurants across London before moving back to his old stomping ground, having grown up near Southwell. He brought a keen interest in the street food scene that was sweeping the capital with him, combining it with his classical training and experience in molecular gastronomy.

The upshot of Edward's move was a place to eat and drink that won Best Food in Broxtowe Borough 2016, and yet is hard to define since it doesn't conform to anything you might expect of street food. Unusual ingredients find a place here, and the evening eight-course tasting menu can transport you from Malaysia to Cambodia via Korea (and a few more stops) if you're adventurous enough to try everything. The mention of Japanese beer, lots of vegetarian food – the kind with tons of flavour, not the kind that's made up of soggy side dishes – alongside lobster and prosecco nights might give you a flavour of what to expect, but the excitement is really in the unknown.

Theatrics to accompany the evening menu, such as aromatic vapour trapped under a glass dome that's released on serving, will delight those with a taste for something different, whilst the lunchtime service focuses on rustic presentation and generous portions, so there's something to suit everyone. The thread that ties it all together at Edward's is the excellence of the staff and the absolute dedication to great food. At its heart, the restaurant has a simple motto (borrowed from Virginia Woolf, and why not, as she puts it so well) – 'One cannot think well, love well or sleep well if one has not dined well.'

Lots of local support has proven that Edward's ethos results in a dining experience people want to repeat, and word of mouth has brought customers from further afield, eager to try something new – a coachload of 20 customers travelled from Huddersfield for an evening meal recently. Now that's an accolade! Edward's is able to go in any direction with the food and drink it serves, unrestricted by theme or cuisine since fusion and fun, both in the kitchen and on the plate, is really the order of the day here, and that makes it a truly exciting place to dine.

Edward's

Edward's
KOREAN BULGOGI 'PHILLY CHEESE STEAK'

The one curveball ingredient in this recipe is a Korean pepper paste called Gochujang. A great secret ingredient to have in the fridge, with pure umami flavour, you can find Gochujang at Asian grocery stores or online. The marinated beef, rancheros peppers, béchamel sauce and warm flatbread spiked with wasabi mayo create a fantastic fusion of flavours.

Preparation time: 1 hour, plus 45 minutes marinating | Cooking time: 1 hour | Serves 1-2

Ingredients

For the bulgogi beef:

900g sirloin steak

3 garlic cloves, minced

½ white onion, diced

3 spring onions, sliced

½ cup soy sauce

2 tbsp sesame oil

3 tbsp dark brown sugar

1 tbsp Gochujang

2 tbsp unsalted butter

2 tbsp olive oil

1 tbsp balsamic vinegar

Salt and pepper

For the rancheros peppers:

1 tbsp olive oil

1 garlic clove, finely chopped

1 small onion, finely chopped

1 tsp smoked paprika

1 large red pepper, finely chopped

1 small red chilli, finely chopped

1 tsp tomato purée

½ tsp ground cumin

400g can chopped tomatoes

For the béchamel:

2 tbsp butter

1 tbsp English mustard

3 tbsp plain flour

285ml milk

250g smoked Applewood cheese, grated

For the flatbread:

50g butter

185ml milk

300g plain flour

½ tsp salt

½ tbsp oil

8 tbsp mayonnaise

3 tsp wasabi

Method

Slice the sirloin very thinly across the grain (we freeze the sirloin for 25 minutes first which makes it easy to cut into very thin strips). Mix all the ingredients for the marinade together and pour over the sliced beef. Refrigerate for 45 minutes.

To make the flatbreads, melt the butter and milk together, then combine with the flour and salt and mix until a sticky dough forms. Sprinkle the work surface with flour and knead the dough for a few minutes until smooth, adding a little more flour if it stays too sticky. Wrap the dough in cling film and rest at room temperature for around 30 minutes.

Using a heavy-bottomed skillet or frying pan over a high heat, add a quarter of the beef along with some of the marinade and toss together as it cooks. After 4 minutes the beef will be medium rare, so adjust the cooking time according to preference.

For the peppers, heat the oil in a medium-sized pan. Add the garlic, onion, paprika, red pepper and chilli and cook over a low heat for 5 minutes. When the onion and garlic are soft but not coloured, turn the heat up and add the tomato purée and cumin. Let the mixture bubble for 1 minute, then add the tomatoes. Cook for 20 minutes over a medium heat. If it begins to dry out, add a little water.

To make the béchamel sauce, melt the butter with the mustard in a saucepan until it comes to the boil. Add the flour and whisk until the mixture has the consistency of breadcrumbs. Add the milk and whisk until all the lumps disappear. Add the grated cheese and whisk again until the sauce has thickened. Add salt to taste.

Divide the flatbread dough into four, form each piece into a ball, then roll out to form rounds of around 0.3cm thickness. Heat the oil in a non-stick pan over a medium heat, and cook the flatbreads one at a time for 1-1 ½ minutes on either side, pressing down gently if they puff up.

To serve

Spread the flatbreads with mayonnaise and wasabi. Lay the strips of cooked bulgogi beef on top, then spoon over the rancheros peppers, and then the hot béchamel sauce. Edward's recommends topping with fried kale, pickled mooli (Chinese radish) and Flying Goose Sriracha Hot Chilli Sauce.

Eat, drink, PARTY!

This family-run, independent business has provided Bridgford with a relaxed daytime eatery as well as a fabulous cocktail bar for evenings out.

Forty Four Bridgford opened its doors in May 2017, beginning life as a bar run by owner Khan Forbes. Robbie and Suki Hohmann joined the team in September 2017, and the bar was relaunched to include food service. With the siblings' combined kitchen and front-of-house expertise, and more importantly the whole team's passion for providing great food, drinks and hospitality, things have moved fast for the ambitious trio, and Forty Four Bridgford now serves freshly made food from morning until evening to much local acclaim, as well as retaining its fantastic cocktail bar and great atmosphere.

Customers can start the day off right with a hearty breakfast of pancakes, waffles, eggs to name a few options, or come for a light lunch, book an afternoon tea including prosecco for that special occasion, or tuck into a delicious meal at dinner time. Using local produce is important for the Forty Four Bridgford kitchen, so companies like Fruit Basket and Nottingham Seafood are valuable suppliers of great ingredients, and local sirloin and lamb feature on the brand new Sunday Roast menu. Robbie aims to make all his menus as affordable and tasty as possible, and Suki complements this with an emphasis on quality table service and a relaxed atmosphere to ensure people leave Forty Four Bridgford happy and looking forward to returning!

Robbie's background has seen him work as sous and head chef at various restaurants around Nottingham, and his enjoyment of catering based on the kind of food he and Suki love to eat led them to set up their other business, Street Food Revolution, just over a year ago. They cater for parties and events on an ad hoc basis and were the first street food vendor to get a nomination for the Nottinghamshire Food and Drink Awards. Running it alongside Forty Four Bridgford, Robbie and Suki agree that they enjoy the best of both worlds with this set-up, which allows them the flexibility to follow their best ideas to suit their varied customer base.

At their cocktail bar and kitchen, the demographic is as diverse as the menu – families are more than welcome, as are those who stay on into the evenings to soak up the party vibes as well as a cocktail or two. The knowledgeable bartenders can shake you up anything from a classic to your very own request, and the in-house DJ is sure to keep you on your feet into the early hours on Fridays and Saturdays. Whether upbeat evenings, lazy mornings or chilled afternoons are what you're after, Forty Four Bridgford want you to love the experience at the cocktail bar and kitchen as much as they love creating it, so you're guaranteed to leave with a smile.

Forty Four Bridgford

INSIDE-OUT CHICKEN WINGS GLAZED IN BLACK BEAN SAUCE, CHILLI AND SESAME

This recipe is a staff favourite at Forty Four Bridgford and popular with the customers too – what's not to love about sticky glazed wings married with punchy Asian flavours? Chef Robbie developed the recipe and uses black bean sauce from authentic oriental food stores.

Preparation time: 45 minutes | Cooking time: approx. 10 minutes | Serves 8-10

Ingredients

2kg chicken wings (ask your butcher to pull the wings through so they are inside out)

990ml black bean sauce

200ml honey

300ml rice wine vinegar

100ml dark soy sauce

150g dark brown sugar

200ml tomato ketchup

30g tomato purée

Vegetable oil, to shallow-fry

Salt and pepper

50g sesame seeds, toasted

3 red chillies, finely sliced

Method

Combine the black bean sauce, honey, rice wine vinegar, soy sauce, sugar, tomato ketchup and purée in a large pan and bring the mixture to the boil, then gently simmer for 8-10 minutes until the sugar is dissolved. Take off the heat and leave the glaze to cool.

Heat the vegetable oil in a deep-sided pan to 170°c using a thermometer probe. When the oil reaches the correct temperature, carefully drop in the chicken wings and shallow-fry until crispy. Use the probe to ensure the chicken reaches 75°c, then remove from the oil and drain on a cloth.

To serve

Warm the glaze back up in the pan, add the cooked chicken and glaze for 2-3 minutes. Finish with the toasted sesame seeds and chilli slices by scattering them over the wings and serve immediately.

Still the catch of THE DAY

This specialist fishmonger on Beeston High Street has a proud history of serving expertly prepared, delicious fresh fish to local customers for over a century.

Fred Hallam Ltd has been a purveyor of fish and game since 1908 and is now presided over by the fourth generation of the Hallam family since the shop's origins. A lot has changed since then, as you might imagine, but the thriving business has remained true to its simple and honest promises, summed up by the slogans printed on a paper bag dating back to the 1950s, which reads: Finest Quality! Fairest Prices! To pay less is risky; to pay more is wasting your money.

Fred Hallam has many suppliers throughout the UK, especially in Cornwall, where the crab and lobster is sourced. These particular favourites are often displayed on the shop's self-serve chiller, dressed and ready to take home to impress guests. The iced display always holds a colourful variety of seafood, including whole fish – plaice, for example – which can be filleted for you at the counter, making finding the perfect ingredients for whatever you're planning to cook easy and fuss free. Sushi fans will want to look out for the Loch Duart salmon; hand-filleted on the premises, the portions are all able to be sold as sashimi grade fish, due to the quality of the product and its preparation.

"From Penzance to Peterhead, we can offer the finest seafood, and when it arrives in the early hours of the morning it is prepared to turn it into fillets and steaks for sale in the store that day." Said owner Miles Hallam.

The fishmonger also holds its own 'Taste of Cornwall' event on the third Saturday of every month – the day of the Beeston farmers' market. A trailer can be seen outside the shop on these occasions, with large turbot and wild bass on the ice, and perhaps a Dover sole being top dressed for a customer by an expert fishmonger. Cornish mussels are popular with customers after a taste of the coastal county, or those on the lookout for tasty paella ingredients, who can pick up Mediterranean prawns, clams and squid too for a transatlantic feast!

And if you're after a treat, current owner Miles Hallam has a few tips up his sleeve for preparing the perfect lobster, after some shop talk with renowned chef Marco Pierre White at a recent food festival. If the prospect of this is a little daunting, Fred Hallam fishmongers will do this to order for you, no knife skills required! But if you do want to get stuck in at home, Miles has laid out a quick guide: Twist the claws off the body and set to one side. With a sharp knife, split the lobster in half from head to tail and remove the thread pipe at the bottom of the tail. Crack the claws with a sharp tap from a heavy knife on both ends, and a quick blow with the back of the knife will reveal the succulent meat. Dip in hot butter or serve with lemon mayonnaise.

Fred Hallam
MEDITERRANEAN HAKE BAKE

This hake bake is simple, healthy but delicious and easy to cook
for the whole family – for four people just double the amount of hake.
I have chosen hake as it's my favourite fish to bake, and is
generally available all year round in our shop. Enjoy!

Preparation time: 15 minutes | Cooking time: approx. 40 minutes | Serves 2

Ingredients

1 red pepper

1 yellow pepper

1 orange pepper

1 medium red onion

250g cherry tomatoes

1 medium parsnip

2 medium courgettes

2 x 200g fillets of hake, skinned and boned

1 tbsp rapeseed oil (we use Yellow Belly)

20g fresh breadcrumbs (10g if using dry)

10-15g Parmesan cheese, grated

2 tbsp parsley, finely chopped

Pinch of sea salt

Balsamic, to dress

Method

Preheat the oven to 200°c. To prepare the vegetables, deseed and slice all the peppers, cut the onion into wedges, dice the parsnip, and slice the courgette into approximately 1cm chunks. Leave the cherry tomatoes whole, and put everything into a large baking tray or ovenproof dish.

Drizzle the vegetables with our Yellow Belly rapeseed oil. Using your hands, mix the veg until it's all coated in the oil. Season with sea salt, and bake in the oven for approximately 20 minutes, or until the vegetables are just charring. Remove the baking tray from the oven, gently turn all the vegetables over and place the hake chunks on top.

Lightly mix the grated cheese and parsley with the breadcrumbs and sprinkle over the fish. Place the tray back in the oven for 15-20 minutes until the fish is cooked through and the breadcrumbs have lightly coloured.

Serve with a generous drizzle of balsamic vinegar.

Spice up YOUR LIFE

The clue's in the name really – Freshly Spiced creates vibrant spice blends and recipe kits for use in home cooking, ground from natural whole ingredients and blended with care for fresh, full flavour.

Freshly Spiced founder Tom, along with his wife Claire, turned a hobby into a livelihood when he realised that, having always been interested in cooking with spices, he was pretty good at creating tasty combinations to suit all kinds of meals, and wanted to ensure that his ideas and hard work weren't spoilt by old spices. Just 20 months in, Freshly Spiced is recommended by Great Food Club, was shortlisted for their Best Producers award and are selling to stockists and commercial buyers as well as flavour-hungry customers.

You don't have to be into chilli to enjoy the subtle, flavourful blends from the Freshly Spiced kitchen though. Some of the mixes are hot – we are talking spices here, after all – but the range of foods they cater for extends far beyond curries, to seafood spaghetti, stews, ice cream and much more. There is a host of ideas, including meal plans and over 30 recipes, for using Freshly Spiced blends on the website, and Tom and Claire plan to keep adding to this archive as they go, as well as their YouTube channel of cooking demonstrations.

All the spices are ground from whole ingredients on a monthly cycle, so customers can rest assured that they're getting really fresh spices every time. Freshly Spiced go a few steps further by toasting the spices to bring out their fullest flavour, bagging the blends by hand and heat sealing the sachets individually. There are currently 15 blends available, as well as individual ground spices, all of which can be bought online – there's even a bi-monthly subscription package!

There are always new ideas in development too, based on seasonal flavours (think burgers on the barbecue in summer, or hot chocolates on cold winter evenings – there are spice blends to complement both of these) as well as inspiration from Tom's family background, where a love of cooking and a focus on great food has been passed down through the generations. From Tom's grandfather owning the first spice shop in Nottingham during the 1950s, to Tom's dad helping him build a production unit in the garden when the business began to expand, there's a definite tradition being drawn at Freshly Spiced.

The business has been doing its bit to educate people about using spices in their cooking too – Tom gives talks about how to get the best flavour out of your spices at home, about healthy eating and about great cooking in general. People's daily lives are busy and home cooking sometimes loses out, but Freshly Spiced aims to provide the basis for fantastically flavourful and fast meals to spice up your everyday.

Freshly Spiced
SPICE INFUSED SCRAMBLED EGGS

This recipe is all about fresh spices designed to beautifully complement good, simple ingredients. The result is a fast, healthy, delicious light supper or exciting brunch.

Preparation time: 10 minutes | Cooking time: approx. 20 minutes | Serves 2

Ingredients

1 onion

3 garlic cloves

1 small chilli (preferably red)

1 red pepper

2 tsp of My Spice Infused Scrambled Eggs blend

Handful of tomatoes

4 eggs

Handful of fresh coriander

Flatbreads, chapatis or toast, to serve

Method

Begin by preparing all the ingredients, as it's a quick-cooking dish. Finely slice the onion and chilli, crush the garlic, roughly chop the pepper and tomatoes and finely chop a handful of coriander. Crack the eggs into a bowl, season with a little salt and pepper and whisk a little.

Now heat a splash of olive oil in a frying pan, and fry the onion until softened. Add the garlic and chilli and continue frying gently. This should take around 8-10 minutes in total.

Add the spice blend and stir for 1 minute, then add the tomatoes and peppers and cook for a further 5 minutes until they have softened. Add the eggs and half of the coriander, leave them to cook for 30 seconds to 1 minute, then begin to scramble them.

To serve

Once the eggs are just scrambled, garnish with the remaining coriander and serve on warmed flatbreads, chapatis or slices of toast.

Around the world in 50 DISHES

The Frustrated Chef brings authenticity and originality to tapas dishes from around the world – the culmination of a shared dream that took some hard knocks before coming to fruition just 18 months ago.

Mattias Karlsson and Patrick De Souza met 14 years ago, and have been working on their vision of bringing something different to the high street restaurant scene pretty much ever since. Their hard work and determination finally paid off when, in February 2016, The Frustrated Chef opened its doors with a waft of the international flavours that have proved irresistible to residents of Beeston, Nottingham, Derby and beyond.

The food that's keeping the tables filled twice over every Friday and Saturday night mainly focuses on Mediterranean tapas, but alongside Spanish and Italian delicacies you'll also find influences from Mexico, Thailand and Morocco – just a few examples amongst many (including Goa, where Patrick grew up) that make for a truly exciting and mouth-watering menu. The specials board is also an important feature in the restaurant, as it changes daily and allows the chefs to 'freestyle' with even more flavour combinations.

As with all great tapas, the dishes are designed to complement one another, so whatever you choose can be eaten as a medley, starting from nibbles to eat indulgently with your fingers, to snacks, salads, fish, vegetarian, meat and dessert options.

Customer favourites reflect the diversity of the offerings, with Korean style belly pork, tiger prawns wrapped in Serrano ham and glazed duck breast with Asian slaw taking the top spots.

Absolutely everything is freshly made in the kitchen, and despite its international outlook, Mattias and Patrick try to source locally where possible, using butchers and greengrocers in Beeston to supply a lot of their ingredients. This laudable approach shows how quickly The Frustrated Chef is becoming a fixture of the area.

You might have been wondering all this time what the story is behind the unusual name of the restaurant – luckily Patrick has revealed that firstly, he has written a book of the same name which documents some of his journey towards opening the restaurant, and secondly, it refers to the setbacks he and Mattias faced in finding the perfect time and place to open The Frustrated Chef. Things fell through on so many occasions that they thought it might never happen – but now that the restaurant is thriving on both its excellent reputation and enthusiastic local patronage, thankfully the two are frustrated no longer!

The Frustrated Chef
TANDOORI MONKFISH WITH AVOCADO MOJO AND LIME SYRUP

Monkfish is a wonderfully meaty fish that holds up to the aromatic spices of the tandoori. Combined with the smooth avocado and piquant lime syrup, this tapas dish is sure to impress your taste buds!

Preparation time: 10 minutes, plus 1 hour marinating | Cooking time: approx. 5 minutes | Serves 4

Ingredients

For the monkfish:

400g monkfish tail, boneless

1 tsp cumin seeds, crushed

2 tsp tandoori masala

½ tsp chilli powder

2 garlic cloves, finely chopped

15g fresh ginger, finely chopped

½ lemon, juice

4 tbsp olive oil

1 tsp salt

½ tsp milled black pepper

For the avocado mojo:

1 small bunch coriander, washed

2 small garlic cloves

2 green chillies, deseeded, chopped

100ml extra virgin olive oil

1 ripe, creamy avocado, peeled and pitted

2 tbsp lemon juice

1 tsp caster sugar

½ tsp salt

For the lime syrup:

2 limes, juiced

2 tbsp caster sugar

½ red chilli, finely chopped

Method

Cut the monkfish into 30-40g medallions and combine with the rest of the marinade ingredients. Leave to marinade in the fridge for at least 1 hour. To make the Avocado Mojo, put all ingredients into a food processor and blend until smooth. For the lime syrup, simmer the lime juice and caster sugar in a small pan for 2 minutes. Leave to cool. Add the chopped red chilli when cool and stir.

To serve

Pan-fry the monkfish medallions for 2 minutes on each side in a non-stick frying pan. Spread the avocado mojo on the plate and arrange the cooked monkfish medallions on top and finish with a drizzle of the lime/chilli syrup.

Best of BRITISH

George's Great British Kitchen provides a unique dining experience in Nottingham city centre, based around classic dishes with unique twists, beautiful design touches and a fun and nostalgic nod to British tradition.

Owners Andrew and Nick are locals through and through, having met each other at primary school and grown up in Nottingham together. The pair developed their unique concept for George's Great British Kitchen out of the absolute British staple, fish and chips, that Andrew's dad George used to serve up at his shop, wanting to bring a classic yet modern dining experience to the city centre.

The food fuses international cuisines that have become so popular in Britain with our own classic dishes – so you might find Atlantic cod cooked in bhaji batter or pea and ham hock fritters with wasabi dip on the menu, for example. Everything is freshly made and developed by George's, where input from the whole team is valued. Attention to detail is a key feature of this restaurant; every small element has been carefully thought about by more than one passionate member of staff. Even the sugar syrups used to create the range of deliciously different cocktails are made in house!

This emphasis on great quality hasn't gone unnoticed – in 2015, George's won Best New Venue at the Nottinghamshire Food & Drink Awards, and in 2016, it won Best City Centre Experience. There is a playfulness mixed in with the ethos that makes George's a really unusual place to dine – you could visit every month and notice something different each time, whether in the décor or on the menu. Fun, inventive touches abound here, particularly in the dessert and cocktail offerings – sweet shop ice cream flavours, candyfloss toppings and Parma Violet or Fab-inspired drinks hark back to childhood memories of British summers at the seaside.

The interior design isn't something you see every day either – from the menus on specially printed newspaper to the beach hut booths named after popular seaside towns, the restaurant is filled with subtle and regionally relevant features that surprise and delight, without being overbearingly novelty. In 2015, George's scooped a 'Heritage' category win in the Bar & Restaurant Design Awards, highlighting the care the company put into restoring the Grade II listed building that houses the restaurant.

It's fun, fresh and subtly quirky, with a focus on quality that ties everything together. From good old fish and chips to highly inventive – and, most importantly, delicious – dishes that embrace a range of international flavours and influences, George's Great British Kitchen absolutely does what it sets out to do.

George's STACKED FISH BURGER

Most of the components of this incredible fish burger can be made ahead of time and assembled whenever you decide to get stuck in! At the restaurant, we use a 'campfire slaw' made with fiery chipotle mayo, and our 'bread and butter pickles' – cucumber and red onion pickled in spiced vinegar and Demerara sugar – along with homemade chips or sweet potato fries, seasoned with the BBQ rub, on the side. Enjoy!

Preparation time: 15 minutes, plus 30 minutes marinating/resting time
Cooking time: 5-10 minutes | Serves 4

Ingredients

4 cod fillets

4 brioche buns

200g polenta

For the BBQ rub:

2 tbsp salt

1 tbsp Demerara sugar

1 tbsp smoked paprika

1 tsp each of garlic powder, onion powder, cayenne pepper and ground black pepper

For the batter:

200g self-raising flour

350g cold water

2 tbsp coriander, roughly chopped

1 tsp chilli flakes

1 tsp salt

1 tbsp malt vinegar

For the toppings:

Pickles of your choice

Coleslaw

Beef tomato, sliced

Mixed salad leaves

Chipotle mayo

Method

Mix all the ingredients for the rub together well; it will make more than you need. Store in a glass jar or an airtight container and bring out for summer barbecues! Cut the fish fillets in half and season well on both sides with the rub. Place on a plate and leave to marinate for 30 minutes in the fridge.

For the batter, combine the water and flour and mix well until it's lump-free. Add the coriander, chilli flakes and salt, mix well and place in the fridge for 30 minutes to rest, or until needed.

If using a fryer, turn on to the highest setting. Get everything ready before starting to cook the fish – working from left to right, place the polenta in a bowl near the fryer. Whisk that all important tablespoon of malt vinegar into the batter, and place the bowl next to the polenta. Place the plate with the fish fillets on the other side of the polenta, and pat dry with kitchen paper to remove any excess moisture. Place a tray lined with kitchen paper to the right of the fryer, to drain the cooked fish on.

Now take a piece of fish and dip it in the batter, drain and toss through the polenta. Repeat with the remaining pieces then place them carefully into the fryer, possibly in two batches depending on the size of your fryer. Fry each fish fillet for a total time of 4 minutes 30 seconds, then lift out of the fryer and drain on kitchen paper.

To serve

While the fish is frying, cut the brioche buns in half and toast lightly, then spread with some of the chipotle mayonnaise. Place some salad leaves over the mayo, followed by a slice of tomato. Place a piece of fish on each tomato slice. Top the fish with a pile of slaw. Top the slaw with another piece of fish. Top this piece with the pickles; take care now the burgers are stacking up! Top each burger with the remaining bun half, securing each with a cocktail stick as you go. Serve as soon as possible, alongside some homemade chips, chipotle mayo and more slaw, then get stuck in!

When two
BECOME ONE

The quiet village of Rolleston can lay claim to a true meeting of East and West – the Gurkha One restaurant serves fine Indian and Nepalese food drawing customers from all over the UK, while the bar area serves real ales, wines and snacks in keeping with the essence of a traditional English pub.

Gurkha One started life in small, rented premises within the city of Nottingham back in October 2014. Founder Jamil had worked in the restaurant trade under various guises (porter, waiter, sous chef, head chef) for years but credits his fiancé, Michaela, and two daughters, Annie and Beth, for encouraging him to launch his own venture. The combination of authentic, quality food made by Jamil – whose mother and grandmother taught him to cook before he trained in the industry – and a personable front-of-house team comprised of Michaela, Annie and Beth saw Gurkha One become very popular, very quickly. Within three months of opening, the restaurant was number one on TripAdvisor in Nottingham and booked up months in advance.

The move to Rolleston in 2015 involved renovating a disused pub and introducing Indian and Nepalese cuisine to the local patrons, but the family 'stuck to their guns' and retained everything about Gurkha One that had proved such a hit, whilst incorporating the village local into their venture. The contemporary décor of the restaurant offsets the traditional English feel of the bar, and the food menu reflects Gurkha One's success in making a whole from two seeming halves, featuring dishes that date back to medieval India as well as newly developed recipes that refine elements of old-fashioned Indian cooking, for example replacing ghee or butter with healthier oils and offering lots of gluten and dairy-free options.

Jamil and his family are proud to acknowledge that Gurkha One is thriving, both as an immensely popular restaurant – still counted amongst TripAdvisor's top five in Nottingham – and a relaxed place to drink, socialise and participate in the bowls, skittles and darts groups that have been carried over from the previous establishment. Three English Curry Awards (Best in the East Midlands as well as Best in the UK in 2015, and Best General Manager for Jamil in 2016), a 2017 Best Restaurant in the East Midlands award, and coming runner-up two years running at the British Curry Awards are well-deserved recognition for the hard work put into create 'something from nothing' as Gurkha One has achieved in such a short time.

Appreciation from visitors all over the UK also means a lot to Jamil, and he enjoys being able to engage with local suppliers to source produce for the restaurant such as vegetables, lentils and even the whole spices thanks to fantastic availability in Nottingham and Leicester. People visit Gurkha One for both the renowned Indian and Nepalese food and the village pub that it incorporates – a marriage of two great things if ever there was one and an experience not to be missed.

Gurkha One
CHICKEN PALUNGO

Palungo is the Nepali word for spinach, so this flavoursome dish is full of bright colour and wonderfully warming layers of spice. The restaurant recommends using chicken thigh rather than breast, for better flavour, and serving with basmati rice and chapatis for a real feast.

Preparation time: 15 minutes | Cooking time: approx. 1 hour 15 minutes | Serves 6

Ingredients

1½kg chicken, thigh or breast

Vegetable oil

5cm piece of fresh ginger, crushed in pestle and mortar

4-6 garlic cloves, crushed in pestle and mortar

2 tsp coriander seeds, crushed

1 tsp ground cumin

2 medium white onions, finely sliced

3 large fresh tomatoes, chopped

2 whole green chillies, sliced

½ tsp mustard seeds

½ tsp paprika

1 tsp garam masala

1 tsp turmeric

Salt and pepper

Bunch fresh coriander, chopped

1kg fresh spinach (palungo)

2 tbsp natural yoghurt

Method

Prepare the chicken by removing any fat, and cut into chunks.

Lightly oil a large pan and add the crushed ginger and garlic. Brown off for 1-2 minutes then add the cumin and coriander seeds, and stir until the seeds start popping.

Add the sliced onion and cook until soft, approximately 8-10 minutes.

Next, add the tomatoes, chillies, remaining spices and half of the chopped coriander. Cover the pan and cook for 15 minutes. If the mixture begins to dry out add a little water.

Ensure the masala has reduced and is hot throughout, then add the chicken and cook the curry over a medium-high heat for about 30 minutes.

Finally, add the spinach and the rest of the chopped coriander (saving a little for garnish) then cover and cook over a low heat for a further 5-10 minutes until the spinach has wilted into the sauce.

To serve

Place a generous portion of the chicken palungo on the plate, served with basmati rice and chapatis. Garnish with the remaining chopped coriander and drizzle with natural yoghurt, then tuck in!

On the
ROAD AGAIN

Contemporary Asian street food, served out of an archetypal American food truck both on the road and at Nottingham Street Food Club, by Masterchef finalist and innovative chef Pete Hewitt.

Pete Hewitt had long nurtured an idea for a venture that centred around great street food, built on Asian influences, to create an exciting eating experience to be enjoyed anywhere. He describes that idea as being 'a bit of a dream' before appearing on the BBC's 2015 Masterchef, but after reaching the finals, making his dream a reality seemed to be a natural progression from the competition. The van, a 1978 Chevrolet stepvan, was purchased in New Jersey and underwent a long conversion process to become the mobile home of Pete's new street food experience, Homeboys.

Homeboys has now been serving great food and drink all over the UK for more than a year, but for lucky Nottingham residents, there's no need to wait for Homeboys to come to you. Homeboys has a fixed premises in the newly refurbished food court in the Victoria Centre's Clock Tower area, which has just reached the six month mark and is proving a popular addition to the informal dining options there. The elements of unity and collaboration in the industry are important to Pete, so having a more permanent residence in Nottingham provides him with an opportunity to focus on the county's

produce and how to best represent the area in his menus, and using fresh bread from Nottingham's The Bakehouse and top-quality meat from Jonny Pusztai is certainly a fantastic place to start.

Pete develops all the menus himself and looks to good ingredients, responsibly sourced, as the basis for creating simple dishes made special. He enjoys the freedom that the travelling aspect of the business allows him, in terms of the regularly changing menu, and doesn't set boundaries in terms of what to try next. Homeboys is fuelled by Pete's passion for an informal eating experience with friends, and supported by his family – mum, dad and brothers are all involved and almost as keen as Pete to ensure the success of this venture. The chef himself is always on the move too, thinking of new ways to do what he does best and stacking up a catalogue of recipes developed in his spare time as he goes. Pete is aiming to open his own restaurant in the near future, so none of these ideas will fall by the wayside, and with such drive behind the wheel of his first street food venture, Homeboys certainly won't either.

HOMEBOYS

2017
BRITISH
STREET
FOOD
AWARDS
FINALIST

Homeboys
DONBURI RICE BOWL

Planning in advance is the key to this dish. There are quite a few little elements involved in the making of it which aren't complicated but need a bit of extra time to make. Homeboys recommends completing your rice bowl with a soft poached egg and steamed pak choi per person, plus garnishes such as crispy shallots, sesame seeds, soy sauce and parsley oil.

Preparation time: 3 hours, plus minimum of 2 hours pickling time| Cooking time: 5 hours | Serves 4

Ingredients

500g Japanese rice

For the pork belly:

1kg piece pork belly

125ml good quality soy sauce

250ml cooking sake

250ml mirin

6 spring onions

6 whole garlic cloves

2 inch piece of ginger

For the relishes and garnishes:

250g daikon

1 tsp salt

250g red miso

3 tbsp mirin

1 inch piece ginger, peeled and minced

500g thinly sliced spring onions

125g ginger, finely minced

60ml vegetable oil

1 tbsp light soy sauce

1 tsp sherry vinegar

1 tsp kosher salt, or to taste

½ tsp monosodium glutamate

50g yuzu kosho paste

300ml olive oil

Method

Roll the piece of pork belly up lengthwise, with the skin facing outwards, and tightly secure at intervals with butchers' twine.

Preheat the oven to 150°c. Heat a cup of water with the remaining ingredients for the pork in a saucepan over a high heat until boiling. Pour the liquid into a deep roasting tin and place the rolled pork belly in the centre (it won't be submerged). Cover with a lid or tin foil. Transfer to the oven and cook the pork for 3 to 4 hours, turning occasionally, until tender – a skewer or thin knife should meet little resistance when pushed into the centre. When done, transfer the contents to a sealed container and refrigerate until completely cool.

To make the miso pickled daikon, peel and slice the daikon into thin rounds, preferably on a mandoline or using a food processor. Toss the slices in 1 teaspoon of salt and leave in a colander over the sink to remove excess water. After 2 hours, rinse off the salt and gently squeeze out the liquid. In a separate bowl, combine the red miso, mirin and minced ginger. Thoroughly coat the daikon in the miso paste mix and place into a sealed container. Leave in the fridge for up to 3 weeks – the pickles will be ready to use after just 2 hours, but will develop more flavour the longer they are left in the mixture. Rinse the miso mix off the pickles before use.

For the ginger spring onion relish, combine the ginger, spring onion, vegetable oil, soy sauce, sherry vinegar, salt and monosodium glutamate in a bowl, stir well, cover with cling film and refrigerate until needed.

For the yuzu kosho oil, simply whisk the yuzu kosho paste with the oil until thoroughly combined and set aside until needed.

Now steam the Japanese rice. Wash the grains until the water runs clear, and soak in fresh water for 30 minutes. Place the rice in a saucepan with a tight-fitting lid, and cover with 560ml water. Bring to the boil on a medium heat, then reduce the heat, cover and leave to cook for 15 minutes without lifting the lid. Remove from the heat and leave to steam, still covered, for a further 10 minutes, then fluff the rice with a fork or paddle and leave for 5 minutes, then serve.

Whilst the rice is cooking, remove the pork belly from the fridge, slice into thin rounds and strain the broth. Sear the pork belly slices on both sides in a frying pan with a tablespoon of rapeseed oil, then ladle some of the reserved broth over pork and reduce until lightly caramelised.

To serve

Place some of the steamed rice in a wide, deep bowl. Lay two slices of the pork on top and a tablespoon of the ginger spring onion relish in the middle. Add the miso pickled daikon and a drizzle of the yuzu kosho oil, followed by two halves of pak choi, a soft poached egg, a large pinch of crispy shallots, a sprinkling of sesame seeds, and a drizzle of the parsley oil if using.

From the heart and
THE HOME

Breakfasts, lunches, cakes and a place to feel welcome – the Homemade Hockley and Pavilion cafés are both bursting with homemade goods, locally sourced and made with real love.

Homemade is a venture that has grown organically from a simple ethos that revolves around cooking proper, honest food for people to enjoy. Jasmin founded Homemade in 2005, when the first café was established in Hockley. She wanted to create a space that could look and feel something like an extension of her own dining room, having regularly cooked for groups of friends around her house, with that same sociable atmosphere that centred on good food, made well.

Hockley Homemade provides a cosy refuge from the busy city, with a focus on cake and coffee – the latter is sourced from a micro-grower in Honduras and a great example of farm-to-table produce – and friendly counter service. Lunch and brunch is also available, though we defy customers not to be tempted by the incredible window display that showcases the beautiful baked goods and other treats made on the premises. This eye-catching smorgasbord of delights changes according to the season and Jasmin's creative flair, which is evident in the café interiors with their quirky antique decorations and vintage touches.

The Pavilion café at the Forest Recreation Ground opened in 2014 after a series of successful pop-ups, and is as light and airy as Hockley is cosy. Jasmin refers to the Forest Rec as an oasis, so close to the centre of Nottingham yet incredibly peaceful. Homemade welcomes walkers from the park, including those accompanied by muddy paws and little ones!

It serves a heartier version of the brunch and lunch menu, with just as many delicious cakes and hot drinks, alongside ice cream for summer days and roast dinners over the winter.

The food menu is developed by Jasmin in collaboration with her team in a process of constant experimentation and learning, especially as they branch out further into vegan and gluten-free options. She describes her staff, including Georgia whom she does the majority of the baking with and Naomi who has worked with her for over seven years, as 'real foodies' with a genuine love for what they produce at Homemade. The whole team have become 'like a family unit' and are trusted by customers who come to Homemade knowing that they can ask exactly what's in the food and get an honest answer. Using local produce is important to Jasmin too, so she has a whole network of suppliers delivering the best of the region directly to the kitchens, as well as being a part of the community of independent businesses who work together to arrange key events, such as the annual Goose Fair, around Nottingham.

Having won awards both locally and nationally, Homemade is the place to go not just for a relaxing and tasty spot of indulgence, but for special occasion catering and spectacular cakes made to order. Sticking with simplicity and bringing people food from the heart has made Jasmin's venture uniquely prized in the city, proving that when it's Homemade, it just tastes better!

Homemade

Apple & Pecan Cake
(w/ apples from jasmin's garden)   4:25

limited edition

Coffee & Walnut Cake ♡

BREAKFAST
LUNCH
& CAKE

Serving locally sourced goodness since 2005.

ROASTED SQUASH & FETA TART

This colourful tart is full of flavour, and can easily be made vegetarian-friendly
with a suitable Parmesan substitute. Ideal for supper served with side salads,
and quick to prepare, especially if you wanted to use shop-bought pastry
(a 500g block of Jus Rol shortcrust pastry would be a good alternative)
in place of making the shortcrust as below.

Preparation time: 45 minutes | Cooking time: 1 hour 30 minutes | Serves 4-6

Ingredients

For the pastry:

100g cold butter, cut into small cubes

80g cold lard, cut into small cubes

350g plain flour

Pinch of salt

4 tbsp cold water, approximately

For the filling:

1 medium-sized butternut squash

1 large red onion

6 large eggs

2 egg yolks

250ml double cream

100g dried Parmesan, grated

1 bunch chives, finely chopped

1 bunch spring onions (just green
ends), thinly sliced

Maldon sea salt and black pepper

200g feta, chopped into small cubes

Olive oil

Method

For the pastry

First, preheat the oven to 180°c. In a bowl, rub the cubes of lard and butter into the flour with your fingertips to make a breadcrumb-like mix. Add a pinch of salt, then slowly add water and bind together until dough forms. It should have a slight stickiness to it. Dust the work surface with flour and roll out the pastry to the thickness of a one pound coin.

Grease a large fluted flan tin and gently lay the pastry over it. Carefully press the pastry into the fluted edges of the tin, making sure the pastry fully covers the sides and edges (don't trim it yet). Cover the pastry with baking parchment, fill with baking beans and blind bake for 15 minutes. Once baked, remove the parchment and baking beans and set aside to cool.

For the filling

Chop the butternut squash into small pieces, place on a baking tray, drizzle with olive oil, season with a sprinkle of Maldon sea salt and pepper, and roast in the oven for 25 minutes. Chop the red onion into chunks, then after 25 minutes add them to the baking tray, mix with the par-cooked squash, and return the tray to the oven for a further 15 minutes.

Meanwhile, whisk the eggs, yolks, cream and Parmesan together in a jug, ensuring that the eggs are fully beaten.

To construct and cook the tart

Once the pastry case has cooled from the blind baking, trim the edges neatly. Scatter the roasted squash and red onion over the base, plus half of the chopped chives and half of the chopped spring onion. Now slowly and evenly pour the egg mix into the pastry case, until it reaches half a centimetre from the top of the tart. Scatter the feta, remaining chives and spring onions over the top. Place the tart into the oven to bake for 30-35 minutes, depending on your oven. You may need to turn the tart around half way through to ensure it is cooked evenly. It will keep cooking on removal from the oven and set fully as it cools.

To serve

The tart should be golden in colour and the filling firm to the touch with a slight wobble. After removing from the oven, wait 15 minutes for the tart to set, then portion up and serve warm.

Homemade
JASMIN'S TOFFEE APPLE CAKE

A note on the ingredients: you can use unsalted butter for the cake batter, but will need to add a pinch of salt if so. The crushed pecans are easily made by taking whole pecans, wrapping them in a cloth or sealable bag, and bashing them with a rolling pin until the desired size. The weight of the apples is taken after peeling and coring.

Preparation time: 30 minutes | Cooking time: approx. 1 hour | Serves 12

Ingredients

For the cake:

250g salted butter, softened

250g soft dark brown sugar

300g self-raising flour

4 eggs

250g apples, peeled and cored

1 tbsp ground cinnamon

1 tbsp ground mixed spice

1 tbsp vanilla extract

For the buttercream:

150g soft butter

200g icing sugar

50ml stem ginger syrup

½ tsp ground ginger

For the toffee drizzle:

150g caster sugar

40g butter

100ml double cream

For the topping:

2 apples, thinly sliced

80g pecans, crushed

1 lemon, juiced

Method

For the cake

Preheat the oven to 170°c then line two 9 inch sandwich cake tins with baking parchment. Place the apples in a saucepan with about 100ml of water over a low heat until softened, then stir in the cinnamon and mixed spice. Set aside.

Using an electric handheld whisk or Kitchen Aid, whip up the butter to a nice smooth consistency, then slowly whisk in the brown sugar. Whisk the eggs and vanilla extract together. Using a sieve, add half of the flour, followed by half of the egg mixture, and mix thoroughly. Do the same again with the remaining flour, and then the rest of the egg mixture, until smooth. Add the spiced apple and fold into the mixture.

Distribute the cake batter evenly between the two sandwich tins; you may need to spread it out with a palette knife or the back of a spoon. Then place in the oven to cook for approximately 35 minutes. Keep an eye on the cakes as times may vary depending on your oven. Once cooked, remove from the oven, leaving the cakes in the tins to cool down for a good hour before icing.

For the buttercream icing

Whisk the butter until smooth and lighter in colour, then whisk in the stem ginger syrup and ground ginger. Using a sieve, gradually add the icing sugar and whisk to a smooth consistency.

For the toffee drizzle

This can be made ahead and stored in a sealable container. In a non-stick saucepan, over a gentle heat, melt the sugar slowly. Do not stir! Once the sugar starts to bubble, add the butter and let it melt through, then stir in the double cream, and set aside to cool and thicken. (Cook's Tip: If your toffee cools too much, it can be gently reheated for 20 seconds in the microwave in a plastic tub!)

To construct

Top the first sponge layer with a generous layer of the ginger buttercream, then sandwich the second sponge layer on top of that, and cover in a thin layer of the buttercream. Top with slices of apple, brushed with lemon juice to stop them browning. Arrange in a fan. Drizzle the cake with toffee, creating a drip effect down the sides. Finish off the cake with some smashed pecans in the centre of the cake, then cut into generous slices, and enjoy!

The true taste of INDIA

An authentic and award-winning restaurant, MemSaab offers Indian fine dining in exquisite surroundings, capturing the essence of traditional and regional cuisine whilst providing visitors from Nottingham and beyond with a modern and enjoyable experience.

Amita Sawhney took on the ownership of MemSaab in 2012, and the restaurant's profile has only risen since that time as the success of this Indian fine dining experience continues. Amita knows how to turn a simple meal with friends or loved ones into a real occasion, and provides a warm welcome front-of-house as well as personal recommendations to diners according to their tastes and spice preferences. MemSaab is a spacious and refined restaurant, sumptuously decorated throughout with a combination of craftsmanship and vibrant modern art. There are two private dining rooms as well, so altogether the restaurant can comfortably seat 200 diners.

It's the perfect setting for a celebratory dinner, and the restaurant can happily cater for large parties and even wedding receptions with its extra bookable space. Each October MemSaab also hosts its own celebrations for the Diwali Festival of Lights, featuring a Pulkha trolley (live cooking station) preparing traditional street food, as well as Rongoli floor art and of course lots of candlelight. Plenty of events draw people in all year round, such as Wine and Food Pairing Evenings and an Annual Charity Evening with twice-Michelin-starred chef Atul Kochhar. Amita is very committed to charity work, having raised more than £145,000 through the restaurant over her years of ownership.

MemSaab's menu showcases a fantastic variety of regional specialities, incorporating irresistible starters and mains featuring lamb, seafood, chicken and even ostrich as well as a host of delicious vegetarian options and desserts. To complement the food, an extended wine list based on months of careful tasting by Amita herself along with local experts is now available, featuring many wines and Champagnes by the glass. All of MemSaab's dishes are beautifully presented, and cooked by talented chefs with regional knowledge from Indian and Pakistan. The team bring traditional methods and individual influences to modern interpretations of Indian cuisine, from Lahore street food to spiced and barbecued meats, capturing both past and present in an accessible and affordable way for everyone who visits the restaurant to enjoy.

The team have certainly cultivated a formula for success, and have created and maintained the restaurant as one of Nottingham's top dining destinations. As well as being featured in the Michelin Guide every year since 2012, MemSaab was also the winner of the Nottinghamshire Food & Drink Best Indian Restaurant Award in 2016, and is proud to be the first and only Indian restaurant in the East Midlands with two AA rosettes. With such a legacy behind it, and Amita at the helm maintaining the focus on excellence as well as, most importantly, an enjoyable experience you'll want to repeat, MemSaab is paving the way for Indian fine dining in the city of Nottingham.

MEMSAAB

MemSaab
GRILLED RACK OF LAMB WITH MASALA SAUCE

In the restaurant, we serve this delicious and elegant dish with mashed potato and blanched baby vegetables alongside the bhaji and Masala sauce for a wonderful fusion of traditional English and Indian flavours.

Preparation time: 20 minutes, plus 2 hours marinating | Cooking time: approx. 45 minutes | Serves 2

Ingredients

For the marinated lamb:

300g New Zealand lamb rack

20g salt

50g deghi mirch (red chilli powder)

50ml lemon juice

1 tsp each garlic and ginger paste

2 tsp sunflower oil

2 tsp yoghurt

For the butter masala sauce:

1 small onion, sliced

10ml olive oil

10g each garlic and ginger paste

2 fresh tomatoes, diced

A few cashew nuts

1 tsp red chilli powder

½ tsp garam masala

Pinch of dry fenugreek

280g paneer (Indian cottage cheese)

1 tbsp butter

100ml single cream 200ml tomato purée

Pinch of salt

For the bhaji:

1 onion, sliced

1 tsp cornflour

1 tsp chick pea flour

1 tsp garam masala

Salt, to taste

Method

Season the rack of lamb and seal on a high heat. Mix the marinade ingredients together and stir well, then cover the sealed lamb rack thoroughly with the marinade and refrigerate for two hours.

To make the butter masala sauce, sauté the sliced onions in olive oil with the ginger and garlic pastes until light golden in colour. Add the tomatoes and cook for another 2 minutes. Add the rest of the ingredients except for the cream and butter. Cover and cook on a slow heat for another 15 minutes, stirring every few minutes. Remove the lid and cook for a further 1 minute on a high heat. Stir in the cream and butter. Take the pan off the heat and blend the sauce into a smooth paste. Season with salt to taste.

Mix the onion bhaji ingredients together and add a little water until a batter forms that coats all the onion slices. Leave to stand for 10 minutes, then fry on a high heat for about 5 minutes, until half cooked. Drain the oil and press the bhaji into a mould. Fry again for one minute just before serving.

Take the marinated lamb rack from the fridge, and cook on a charcoal grill for 8-10 minutes, turning over every minute, until cooked but pink inside.

To serve

Place the rack of lamb on the plate with the onion bhaji to one side, and finish with the butter masala sauce. If you like, top the bhaji with mashed potato, place some sautéed baby vegetables, such as corn and carrots, to the side, and garnish with fresh herbs. Enjoy!

A very worthwhile INVESTMENT

Chris and Gosia are passionate about wine and want to bring the best customer service to their business, focusing on finding quality wines at the best value for money in friendly and relaxed surroundings.

The Wine Bank is a relatively recent addition to the town of Southwell, having opened in 2014 when owners Chris and Gosia set up Mr & Mrs Fine Wine. 2016 saw an expansion into new, bigger premises for The Wine Bank, providing an opportunity not only to expand the range but also to allow customers to come and drink the wines in a beautifully refurbished 19th century building. 'The bank (which previously occupied the building, hence Chris and Gosia's name for the shop) literally walked out and left everything behind, sadly except the money, so we had to strip back almost to the bricks, but it did give us the opportunity to create something very unique.'

The Wine Bank is a hybrid; both a wine shop and a wine bar featuring wines from all over the world, many of which are imported directly by Chris and Gosia. Customers can use the exciting Vault Machines to pour themselves a taste of the wines available – a unique way to get a sense of the wines before buying them. It's easy to lose yourself in the great array of wines on offer, whilst sipping at a fine wine hand-selected for you by the team at The Wine Bank, in the friendly and relaxed atmosphere of a wine bar. With over 450 wines, spirits, beers and liqueurs, there's certainly plenty to peruse, and if you're feeling peckish, the cheese, charcuterie and olive platters at The Wine Bar are a perfect accompaniment.

The Wine Bank team are always looking for new and interesting wines, but also like to find wines from recognised areas that are offering real value and classic styles. "People really enjoy the wines we find and are also keen to try new wines that we continually bring in." For customers, it's refreshing and reassuring to be able to come into The Wine Bank and sense the excitement and passion that the team have for their wines, and take advantage of the extensive knowledge they are happy to share.

The Wine Bank also works with local restaurants to supply their wine lists, and can help with wedding and event wines as well as corporate gifts. The busy schedule includes regular tasting events too in the rather splendid Treasury Room – from gin and wine masterclasses to personalised tastings for individual customers and groups, there are fun and enjoyable options available for all occasions at this unique and welcoming shop and bar.

Our wine pairings and
GUIDELINES

The challenge of pairing food and wine can be a baffling task, however, there is such variety in grapes and wine styles that you can be sure of finding something to match your food choice. We have outlined a few guidelines and paired some specific recipes from this book with our wines below, which we hope will enhance your dining experience. Remember that at the end of the day, though, it's all about picking a wine you enjoy – look to source wines from independent businesses like us, where you can find expert advice and guidance.

Have fun! – Chris & Gosia

Pinot Noir: Silky, Smooth and Sensual

A medium red with red cherry, raspberry and even cranberry characters depending on where it is from. Pinot Noir can have good acidity which makes it pair well with lamb, pork and tomato-based dishes as well as ingredients like mushrooms and roast vegetables. Don't forget, a meaty fish dish works well with a light balanced Pinot Noir too! Pinot Noir can have an earthy Old World style, as in those from Burgundy, France, or it can have a more fruit-forward, New-World style.

Warramate Pinot Noir – Yarra Valley, Australia with Three Bean Soup with Chorizo (Toast)

Handley Pinot Noir – Anderson Valley, California, USA with BBQ Pulled Pork (Thaymar Ice Cream, Farm Shop & Tea Room)

Domaine Remoriquet – Bourgogne Pinot Noir – Burgundy, France with Extraordinary Pork with Starkey Bramleys (Starkey's Fruit)

Chardonnay: Rich and Complex to Light and Crisp

This wine can be very versatile when pairing with foods. Oaked Burgundies with creamy nutty notes pair beautifully with white meats like chicken, pork and veal, delicious meaty fish like salmon and lobster, and even vanilla-based desserts. Younger, leaner unoaked chardonnays, from cooler climates like Tasmania, offer up crisp, citrus characters which lend themselves to more delicate seafood, fresh vegetable dishes and especially creamy sauces.

Domaine Moingeon – St Aubin, Premier Cru – Sur Gamay, Burgundy, France with Lime and Coconut Cake (Tiffin Tea House)

Holm Oak, Chardonnay – Tasmania with Roasted Mediterranean Vegetable and Goat's Cheese Quiche (Mulberry Tree Café)

Domaine Alexandre, Chablis – France with Lobster Mac 'n' Cheese (Colston Bassett Dairy)

Champagne & Sparkling: Excellent Food Wine

Often associated with celebrating special occasions, sparkling wine can come in a variety of styles. With its natural acidity, a Champagne is perfect with salty or creamy foods like oysters and creamy fish dishes. Budget doesn't stretch to Champagne? Try a Crémant instead, a Champagne in all but name and a great alternative. Prosecco also works wonderfully well as an aperitif and can also pair fabulously with certain desserts.

Domaine du Landreau, Cremant de Loire – France with Lime and Coconut Cake (Tiffin Tea House)

Coates & Seely, Brut Reserve NV – England with Eggs Benedict (The Clock House)

Champagne Henriot, Brut Souverain – France with Lobster Mac 'n' Cheese (Colston Bassett Dairy)

Nani Rizzi Valdobbiadene Prosecco Extra Dry DOCG with Ridiculously Easy Fresh Ricotta Malfatti and Sage Butter (Welbeck Farm Shop)

Cabernet Sauvignon: Big, Bold & Beautiful

With layers of flavour full of fruit and tannin, this is another grape that can come in a variety of styles. New World cabernets tend to be more fruit-forward with blackcurrant and cassis characters, where Old World examples tend to be drier, smokier and tannic. The taste of berries can liven up hearty dishes like casseroles and stews, and drier cabernets can complement roast red meats and steaks. A big, bold Bordeaux wine with roast beef is a classic pairing.

Château Sorbey, Haut-Medoc – Bordeaux, France

Bodega Sottano, Cabernet Sauvignon – Mendoza, Argentina with BBQ Pulled Pork (Thaymar Ice Cream, Farm Shop & Tea Room)

Vina Robles, Cabernet Sauvignon Estate – Paso Robles, California, USA

Sauvignon Blanc: Crisp and Refreshing

Styles range from steely French Sauvignons with a great minerality – to pair with shellfish, seafood and sushi – to big, aromatic New World Sauvignon packed full of tropical fruit and gooseberry. The common factor is crisp, lively acidity that means you pair a Sancerre with green vegetables and goats cheese on the one hand, and a Sauvignon Blanc from Marlborough, New Zealand with lightly spiced Asian cuisine on the other.

Hawksdrift, Marlborough Sauvignon Blanc – New Zealand with Roasted Mediterranean Vegetable and Goat's Cheese Quiche (Mulberry Tree Café) or Extraordinary Pork with Starkey Bramleys (Starkey's Fruit)

Domaine Balland, Sancerre, Croq'caillotte – France with Lime and Coriander Cured Salmon with Avocado, Spinach and Poached Egg on Sourdough (Cartwheel Café)

Flametree Sauvignon Blanc/Semillon – Margaret River, West Australia with Lobster Mac 'n' Cheese (Colston Bassett Dairy)

Dry Rosé: Perfect Pairing All Year Round

Don't limit yourself to rosé only in the warmer months, although it does work fabulously well with light summer salads. Why not try rosé with a cheese soufflé, fish cakes or paellas? These low tannin wines really do lend themselves to a number of foods like mussels and fish, and not just to an aperitif in the sunshine.

Château Saint Pierre, Cuvee Tradition – Cotes de Provence, France with Roasted Mediterranean Vegetable and Goat's Cheese Quiche (Mulberry Tree Café)

Domaine Balland, Les Beaux Jours Rosé – Coteaux du Giennois, France with Lobster Mac 'n' Cheese (Colston Bassett Dairy)

Malbec: Vibrant with Attitude

This grape has become synonymous with Argentina, but actually originates from France. The wines tend to have a big, bold character full of black fruits like blackcurrants and plums, and Malbec tends to be less tannic than Cabernet Sauvignon. A super wine, with great versatility – partners exquisitely with foods ranging from traditional Argentine steak, for heavy Malbecs, to pizza and spaghetti Bolognese, for lighter style Malbecs.

Bodega Sottano, Seleccion, Malbec – Mendoza, Argentina with Wagyu Beef with Raw Beef Taco and Burnt Hotdog Onions (The Black Bull)

Château de Chambert, Malbec – Cahors, France with Frying Pan Pizza (The Rustic Crust)

Syrah/Shiraz: Full of Berries and Spice

Syrah or Shiraz are actually the same grape but are named differently depending on where you are. An Australian Shiraz from the warmer climates tends to be rich and full-bodied, whereas a Rhone Valley Syrah can have a touch of spice and minerality to it. Both pair well with bold foods, as the punch of flavour from the warmer climate wines works fantastically with barbecued meats, whereas a cooler climate Syrah marries well with grilled meats, aubergines and Middle Eastern spiced food.

Bramble Lane Shiraz – Rosabrook, Western Australia with BBQ Pulled Pork (Thaymar Ice Cream, Farm Shop & Tea Room)

Domaine des Amphores, Les Iris, Syrah – France with Aubergine Parmigiana Pie (Vork Pie)

Kaesler, Old Vine Shiraz – Brossa Valley, Australia with South Carolina BBQ Pork Belly Bites (Sauce Shop)

A lunchtime RETREAT

Mulberry Tree Café is a wonderfully relaxing spot for a long lunch, afternoon tea or light bite that makes the most of its beautiful surroundings at Strelley Hall just outside Nottingham.

Even locals could be forgiven for not knowing of Strelley Hall's existence, tucked away as it is at the end of a lane of cottages. The old stables right next door underwent the transformation to become Mulberry Tree Café almost three years ago. Owner Geraldine Rudham and Manager Dawn Martin have since developed Mulberry Tree Café into a popular destination for anyone looking for a pretty, relaxing spot for a bite to eat conveniently located just outside the city but located in gorgeous countryside. There are even guided walks that end in the café with lunch or afternoon tea run in association with the Woodland Trust, while the Broxtowe Country Trail runs close by the café so cyclists and walkers can pop in for some much-needed refreshment.

Geraldine grew up in Strelley and her parents run Strelley Hall as a business and events centre, so she knows the ins and outs of the area – and the quirks of the estate itself – better than most. The 'Museum Pen' in the café houses information about the beautiful historic buildings and some fascinating finds from the grounds. There are old photographs and transcripts of old letters on the walls too, detailing the lives of characters such as the fierce Squire Edge and Mr Skinns, the rather threateningly named butler.

The café itself features booths fashioned out of the original stalls of the stables, the tack room is now the kitchen, and the governess' pony used to be kept in what is now the toilets! The name and the colours of the café allude to a very old mulberry tree that stands in the grounds of Strelley Hall, which still bears fruit today – mulberry cheesecake and other autumnal delights have featured on the menu each year when harvest time comes around.

Warming soups, freshly made quiches, home cooked daily specials and cakes from the on-site bakery are made from locally sourced ingredients where possible, with gluten-free and vegetarian options always available too. The café also serves loose leaf teas in infuser pots for those partial to a cuppa with a bit of refinement, as well as a unique blend of coffee created especially for the café.

Mulberry Tree Café really deserves the somewhat clichéd designation 'hidden gem' – this one is certainly worth seeking out, to make a day of the lovely surroundings and more importantly, the delicious food!

Mulberry Tree Café

Mulberry Tree Café

ROASTED MEDITERRANEAN VEGETABLE AND GOAT'S CHEESE QUICHE

This delicious quiche was developed by the kitchen staff and has become a real favourite with customers. At Mulberry Tree Café, they cut it into 6 generous slices for serving, but it can serve 8-10 for a light lunch. A good quality goat's cheese will make a big difference to the overall flavour.

Preparation time: approx. 1 hour, plus 1 hour chilling | Cooking time: approx. 4 hours | Serves 8-10

Ingredients

For the pastry:

300g plain flour

Pinch of salt

70g vegetable shortening (Trex, for example)

70g butter

40ml cold water to mix

For the quiche:

500g Mediterranean vegetables (peppers, courgettes, aubergines, red onions, cherry tomatoes all work well)

65g firm goat's cheese

350g cheddar cheese

1 medium onion, diced

1 tbsp olive oil

5 eggs

125ml double cream

Salt and pepper

Method

Mix the flour and salt in a large bowl. Rub in the fat. Add the water and using a round-bladed knife, cut and stir until the mixture comes together to form a stiff dough. Wrap the pastry in cling film and rest it in the fridge for at least an hour, or until needed.

Using a 28cm deep quiche tin with a removable base, roll out the pastry until it is about 6-7cm larger in diameter than the quiche tin. It should be about half a centimetre thick. Fold the pastry over a rolling pin and lay it over the tin. Gently push the pastry into the corners and leave the excess hanging over the sides of the tin. Place the tin on a baking sheet and prick the pastry base all over with a fork, then cover with a large piece of baking parchment and fill with ceramic baking beans. Bake at 160°c for 30 minutes, then uncover and bake for a further 5-10 minutes until the pastry is golden brown. Leave to rest at room temperature while preparing the filling.

First prepare the vegetables. Slice the courgettes, aubergines and onions, halve the tomatoes, and cut the peppers into a large dice. Roast the vegetables at 180°c with olive oil and seasoning until cooked through. This should take approximately 45 minutes but will depend on the vegetables used.

Next, fry the onion in olive oil until soft. Mix the eggs with the double cream and add salt and pepper. Grate the cheddar cheese and cut the goat's cheese into small dice.

Layer the fried onion, goat's cheese, roasted vegetables and about two thirds of the cheddar cheese into the pastry case. Add half of the egg mixture and mix carefully. Then pour on the rest of the egg mixture, and sprinkle the remaining cheddar over the top. Bake the quiche at 160°c for about 1 hour, until the top is golden brown and the filling is cooked through and set, without too much of a wobble.

To serve

When the quiche has cooled to room temperature, cut into slices and serve on plates garnished with a light green salad.

All ABOARD

Mark Osborne and David Hage have put The Railway Lowdham right on track since its complete refurbishment in March 2017, giving villagers a local to be proud of with fantastic food, drink and events that everyone can enjoy.

Dating back to 1876 in some parts, the building that underwent such a momentous renewal earlier this year to become The Railway Lowdham has always been a pub in one form or another. Mark and David, who together comprise The Secret Pub Company, found the place in need of a little TLC when they began their quest to reinstate the quintessential village pub. The grand reopening was a year in the making, but it seems as though it was all worth it for the co-owners who admit to being 'in love with the place'.

The concept for the refurbished pub was somewhere locals would proudly show off to visiting friends and family, a place that provided for families and real ale enthusiasts alike, and one that hosted exciting events so that something new and inviting was always going on. The menu reflects this, being seasonally dependent, with tweaks made every 5-6 weeks through input from the whole team – a close-knit and experienced bunch who have worked with Mark and David before – to ensure the best locally supplied produce is always being showcased.

Great food is of course complemented by great wine, courtesy of a unique supplier. They also have five cask ales and a choice of over 30 gins, so whatever your tipple, you're well looked after. Cosy fires and conversation are the order of the day in the bar, where live music every Friday night enhances the atmosphere, as does the intriguing interior design with its nod to the pub's heritage – the seating is constructed from antique suitcases on an original railway track.

Visitors are already starting to come from further afield as the fledging pub's reputation travels from county to county, just as Mark and David wanted. The ambitious duo is already considering taking another venue under The Secret Pub Company's wing, alongside ensuring lasting success at their first labour of love, The Railway Lowdham. Opening early to serve coffee, with a lunch menu, outdoor space for children's play and al fresco dining on top of the evening food and entertainment, The Railway Lowdham seems to have hit on a winning formula for engaging the local community, and looks likely to become a runaway success.

ROAST CORNISH HAKE WITH GIROLLE MUSHROOMS, FRESH PEAS, CREAMED POTATO, AND ROAST CHICKEN SAUCE

This recipe should bring out the purest, most intense flavours in the ingredients – a straightforward combination but one that produces very tasty results! Chef Mark Osborne has a tip for those without a reliable non-stick pan: use a piece of greaseproof paper to cook the fish on in the hot pan.

Preparation time: 30 minutes | Cooking time: approx. 4½ hours | Serves 4

Ingredients

1kg chicken wings

1 leek, cleaned and chopped

1 carrot, peeled and chopped

2 shallots

3 garlic cloves

1kg potatoes, peeled

150g unsalted butter

50ml double cream

4 x 220g portions hake, or other white fish

100g girolle mushrooms

4 tbsp fresh peas

2 spring onions, chopped

Lemon juice, to taste

1 tbsp parsley, chopped

Sea salt and ground pepper

Method

To make the roast chicken sauce, start by placing half of the chicken wings into a deep oven tray. Roast the wings in a preheated oven at 180°c for 1 hour, turning every ten minutes, until they are a golden colour. Place the rest of the wings in a large pot and cover with cold water. Bring up to the boil, and skim off any fats that have risen to the surface. Add the leek, carrot, shallots and garlic and simmer for 2 hours. After the 2 hours, remove the wings and all the vegetables and then add the roasted wings to the stock. Rapidly reduce the liquid by half then take out the wings. Continue to reduce until you have a thickened sauce, and set aside.

Next, chop the peeled potatoes into large pieces and place into a suitable saucepan, cover with water and season with a little salt. Boil the potatoes until just cooked, and drain off the cooking water. Let them stand for 2 minutes to steam dry, then pass the potato through a fine sieve or a potato ricer back into the pan. Add half the butter and half the cream to the riced or sieved potato, work the mixture with a spatula until smooth and season with salt and pepper.

For the hake fillets, preheat a non-stick frying pan until it's hot but not smoking, then add a little oil and place the hake fillets skin side down in the pan (on greaseproof paper if using). Cook until a little colour has appeared, then turn the heat down and cook for a further 2-3 minutes. Flip the fillets over and cook for a further for 2 minutes. The fish should be slightly opaque when cooked, so remove from the heat at this point and season with sea salt.

Next, heat a small saucepan with a little olive oil and the remaining unsalted butter in. Once the butter has started to foam, add the girolle mushrooms and cook for 1-2 minutes, stir in the chopped spring onions and peas, season with a few drops of lemon juice and add the chopped parsley.

To serve

Warm through all the separate elements of the dish and have four warm plates ready. Spoon equal quantities of the creamed potato onto each plate, place a fillet of fish on one side, spoon over the mushrooms, and finish with the chicken sauce.

It's all about THE DOUGH

The Rustic Crust are all about authentic, Neapolitan style wood-fired pizza served from a converted Land Rover – Poppy the pizza truck – and are based in Nottingham but ready for any occasion!

The Rustic Crust team pride themselves on their authentic Neapolitan-style dough, which forms the crucial crust (of course) and base of the pizzas which are always made fresh to order. Husband and wife team Ross and Camille have over 12 years' pizza making experience, but more importantly, a great love and passion for what they do.

After stumbling across an inspirational pizzeria in Rome, on the couple's return to the UK, Ross began building his first traditional Pompeii pizza oven and his quest to make proper pizza. Three homebuilt ovens later, Ross and Camille are now sharing the results of this quest with a wide and enthusiastic audience. Poppy the pizza truck, named by their daughter Lucy, is a converted Land Rover defender and the core of Ross and Camille's business. Over the last three years, The Rustic Crust has been serving proper pizza at weddings, corporate events, parties, pop-ups and VIP catering from Poppy's Neapolitan oven up and down the country, and has built up a fabulous, friendly and loyal customer base who refer to themselves as 'pizza stalkers' – some are so devoted they even bring their own containers for the Parmesan cream!

The dough is always hand-pushed and hand-tossed: not a dough roller or frozen dough ball in sight. The quality and freshness of the ingredients used, from the homemade Italian Sausage (salssiccia picante) to that infamous Parmesan cream, set The Rustic Crust apart in an industry where there's a lot of competition amidst the street food trends sweeping the country. Genuine pizzaioli (pizza-makers) have a love for their craft, and as per Ross and Camille's ethos, quality will always come first for those people, meaning more customers get to taste proper pizza that should be light, easy to digest, well-seasoned and with real depth of flavour.

The Rustic Crust method advocates a wood-fired oven (used properly) as the very best way to cook pizza, but also acknowledge that cooking methods are only part of the story. Neapolitan pizza is all about the dough and cooking quality ingredients to perfection. For those at home without wood-fired ovens capable of reaching around 500°c, Ross and Camille recommend using a non-stick frying pan and a preheated grill (this is also a great way to reheat pizza). The intense heat of the grill and the frying pan together will cook the toppings, and more importantly create steam from the moisture in the dough, which will puff up the pizza edge, and give you the perfect 'Rustic Crust' or cornicione.

This obsession with pizza dough is attracting a string of admirers as well as awards, recently making it into the regional finals for the highly-acclaimed Wedding Industry Awards.

So, why not have a go at the recipe overleaf and share some proper pizza love on social media @therusticcrust or visit us online at www.therusticcrust.co.uk.

FRESH · WOOD-FIRED · PIZZA

The Rustic Crust

The Rustic Crust
FRYING PAN PIZZA

Because our house method and dough recipe isn't easy to recreate at home,
we've put together a really simple dough recipe that we use at
The Rustic Crust to test flavour combinations – it's robust, quick to make,
and (with some practice) easy to handle and shape.

Preparation time: 30 minutes, plus 17-24 hours proving | Cooking time: 5 minutes | Makes 8 x 10" bases

Ingredients

1kg 00 tipo flour

3g dried yeast

550ml of water, at room temperature

25g fine sea salt

Method

Pour the water into a large bowl and dissolve the yeast in it, then leave to stand for 5 minutes. Slowly add the flour, folding it in gently with your hands. When the mix comes together, turn it out and knead the dough for 5 minutes, then stretch out the dough, sprinkle over the salt and continue to fold and stretch for another 5 minutes. Shape the dough into a large ball and cover with a damp cloth. Leave to rest on the work top for 15 minutes. After resting, knead the dough for 30 seconds and shape back into a large ball. Leave to rest at cool room temperature in an airtight container for 12-16 hours.

Now divide the dough into 220g portions. With the palm of your hand, gentle pressure and a soft grip, roll each portion in an anti-clockwise circle to create a tight ball. Place the dough balls on a baking tray or worktop and cover with a damp cloth to prove for 5-8 hours. On a well-floured surface, generously flour the top of the dough ball and using your fingertips slowly push out from the centre of the dough, leaving a centimetre rim around the edge to create the 'rustic crust' of the pizza, called the cornicione in Naples. Flip the dough ball over and repeat with more flour, using the palms and backs of your hand to stretch the dough.

To cook the pizza, make sure all the pizza toppings are prepared and close to hand, then preheat the grill to the highest setting and heat a non-stick, dry frying pan until it's very, very hot but not smoking. Slide the pizza base into the hot pan. Add the sauce first and any toppings, leaving a good inch clear around the edge. Cook for around two minutes over high heat. Now place the frying pan under the hot grill. Keep checking the pizza. Depending on the chosen toppings (remember less is more) and on how well done you like your pizza crust, it will be cooked in approximately 2-3 minutes. Slice up, serve and enjoy!

Recommended Pizza Toppings

Prosciutto, mushroom, and an egg with garlic cream ricotta.

To make the garlic cream ricotta, mix 500g ricotta cheese with 1-3 teaspoons of minced fresh garlic, a little olive oil, salt and pepper to taste and full-fat milk or cream to thin the mixture and create a sauce-like consistency. Add the egg just before you put the pizza under the grill and the other toppings as stated in the recipe.

Bottled at SAUCE

From the kitchen of their own home and cold mornings at farmers' markets, to premises in a former lace factory and over 250 stockists, Pam and James Digva have taken their range of sauces to new heights, whilst retaining everything that makes Sauce Shop such a unique and tasty business...

Almost four years ago, Sauce Shop began with a small idea, based around the trend for interesting and authentic condiments that fought back against bland brands filling supermarket shelves. Since then, the business has grown exponentially and exciting developments are not just on the horizon, but on the doorstep for the team of family and friends fighting for real sauce. Husband and wife James and Pam have been joined by Pam's brother Ali, who's in charge of getting the word out there, as well as Ali's friend Nathan, who heads up production, and James' nephew Kyle, who's still learning the ropes.

In 2014, when Sauce Shop featured in the first Nottingham Cook Book, it had nine retailers for the product range. There are now over 250 stockists selling Sauce Shop products across the UK, including big names like Whole Foods Market, Harvey Nichols and Daylesford Organic, with Harrods very soon to join the starry line-up. There is a full list of stockists on Sauce Shop's website, including an online store, so wherever you are, you need never run out of your favourite sauce!

Both James and Pam have backgrounds in food manufacturing, which allowed them to develop a strong ethos in terms of what they did and didn't want in their own sauces. Unnecessary additives, thickeners, and watering down are all on the naughty list, so the sauces themselves are pretty much just fruit and vegetables and have incredible depth of flavour as a result, evidenced by the five Great Taste awards they've scooped in 2017 alone.

It's a busy year for Sauce Shop, who will be making an appearance at the BBC Good Food show in November, alongside plenty of local Christmas markets. A new range of aged hot sauces is launching soon, and the newest White Label flavour (a play on limited edition vinyl records and Sauce Shop's quirky Dymo label branding) to look out for is Pumpkin Hot Sauce!

The business that grew out of one kitchen in Nottingham is certainly doing the city proud as it expands both in reputation and customer base across the country, but also stays true to its roots by using local companies where possible and, most importantly, by hand crafting every kettle-load of sauce to ensure unrivalled quality. What a lot of bottle!

It's all in THE SAUCE

Since starting up our business three years ago, our range has grown from just 7 sauces to nearly 17 products including sauces, mayonnaises and special limited editions. We hope you enjoy using them with or in your home cooking.

Ketchups and BBQ Sauces

Of course, the main use for our ketchups and BBQ sauces is as a condiment, but many of them can be used in cooking as a marinade or flavour enhancer. Our South Carolina and Korean BBQ sauces work really well on pork, especially used as a marinade for belly or ribs, and you have to try a bit of brisket that's been drenched in our Smoky Chipotle Ketchup! For the less adventurous cook, we recommend simply adding a big splodge of any of our ketchups to your plate. Our mushroom ketchup, which is based on a traditional condiment recipe, is especially good on anything featuring sausages, bacon and eggs! And we can't omit a mention of our Tomato Ketchup – unlike any ketchup you've tasted before, it has an intense tomato hit that often converts people from the big brands.

Chilli and Hot Sauces

From our Lime and Coriander Sauce, which has just a hint of green chilli, to our Habanero aged hot sauce, our range has something to suit everyone including absolute beginners and established chilli fans. Smother fried chicken wings with our Buffalo Hot Sauce, and coat chicken strips with our Green Sriracha to give fajitas an extra lift. Our brand new range of aged hot sauces go through a special fermentation process to produce an extra savoury flavour. Although James would argue that these go with everything, Pam recommends trying the Original Hot Sauce in a burrito! Not to be forgotten, our Great Taste award-winning red Sriracha can add a hot, sweet and savoury kick to most dishes.

Mayonnaise

After deciding mayonnaise needed the Sauce Shop treatment, James set to work developing a range that would bring homemade mayo to shop shelves. Our original mayo is based on a Japanese recipe, containing rice wine vinegar and using only egg yolk for extra richness. There are also two flavoured mayonnaises in the range, spiked with our Smoky Chipotle and Sriracha sauces. Chipotle Mayo is a staple in Pam and James' house – great used as a dip for pizza, or as a burger sauce – and team members Ali and Nathan can often be seen consuming large plates of sweet potato fries covered with our Sriracha Mayo.

Limited Editions

2017 has seen the introduction of our seasonal limited edition flavours, identified by their white label. There are always loads of ideas flying around the Sauce Shop office, so we decided to create an outlet for them. So far we've launched a Habanero Ketchup – each bottle containing 22 Habanero chillies (not for the faint-hearted) – and a Cherry Bourbon BBQ sauce. Next up is a spiced Pumpkin Hot Sauce, perfect for warming you up in the colder months. We can't wait for what's ahead in Sauce Shop's busy calendar, and we hope you feel the same way after trying our unique products.

Sauce Shop
SOUTH CAROLINA BBQ
PORK BELLY BITES

The BBQ sauce is the star of the show here, adding tangy and sweet notes with a hint of smoke to the meat. This indulgent but enjoyably low-maintenance recipe works brilliantly with Sauce Shop's Korean BBQ Sauce too.

Preparation time: 10 minutes | Cooking time: approx. 4 hours 10 minutes | Serves 3-4

Ingredients

Between 1 and 1½kg pork belly

Vegetable oil

2 tbsp brown sugar

1 tbsp salt

100g butter, diced into 1cm cubes

150ml South Carolina BBQ sauce

Method

Preheat the oven to 120°c. Ideally use a thick piece of pork belly. Remove the skin and cut the pork into approximately 4cm cubes and place in a large roasting tin. Pour over enough oil to coat all of the meat and then sprinkle over the salt and half of the sugar. Massage this in with your hands so the meat is evenly coated.

Place the roasting tin in the preheated oven and cook the pork for 2 hours. After this time, the meat should be browned on the outside and most of the fat will have rendered out into the roasting tin. Turn the meat with tongs, sprinkle with the remaining brown sugar and tuck the cubes of butter between the pieces of pork belly.

Cover the tin with foil and return to the oven for another 2 hours, turning the cubes of meat every 30 minutes. Take the roasting tin out of the oven and remove the foil, pour off as much of the fat as possible and turn the oven up to 200°c. Add the South Carolina BBQ Sauce to the tin, glazing all of the meat. Return the tin to the hot oven for 5-10 minutes, which will brown the edges of the meat and set the sauce.

To serve

Serve the cubes on their own as a nibble, or with fries, slaw and pickles for a slap-up meal.

Sauce Shop
SRIRACHA FRIED CHICKEN

Sriracha sauce is named after the coastal city of Si Racha in eastern Thailand, thought to have been originally created to go with seafood. Sauce Shop's award-winning version is made with fermented red chillies and garlic, and paired here with fried chicken to create an indulgent treat with a kick.

Preparation time: 5 minutes, plus at least 6 hours marinating | Cooking time: 30 minutes | Serves 3-4

Ingredients

150ml Sriracha

200ml buttermilk

1kg chicken pieces (wings, thighs, drumsticks, or breast halves)

Enough vegetable oil to fill your saucepan to a depth of about 8cm

300g plain flour

Salt

Method

Combine the Sriracha and buttermilk in a large bowl, then add the chicken pieces and mix to ensure each one is well coated. Cover with cling film and refrigerate for at least 6 hours, or preferably overnight.

Heat the oil in a large pan to 175°c. Season the flour with a good pinch of salt in a large bowl. Remove the chicken from the marinade and dredge in the flour, ensuring each piece is fully covered. Shake off any excess and transfer to a plate.

Carefully add the chicken to the hot oil with tongs, in batches if necessary so the pan isn't crowded. After 5 minutes, turn the chicken pieces. Continue to do this every few minutes to ensure even browning. After 15-20 minutes the chicken will be well browned and cooked through. The larger the pieces, the longer they will take to cook.

If possible, use a meat thermometer to check the internal temperature of the chicken, which should be 75°c.

Take the chicken out of the pan and transfer to a cooling rack set over a tray lined with paper towels. If cooking in two batches, put the first batch into an oven preheated to 130°c to keep it warm. Let the fried chicken sit for 2-3 minutes, before serving with extra Sriracha or Sriracha mayo on the side!

Springing INTO ACTION

After a major refurbishment of the shop, butchery and bakery, all three generations of the family-run Spring Lane Farm Shop are eager to embrace a new era of their business.

The Spencer family are enthusiastic about the new look of their recently refurbished farm shop, which grew out of humble beginnings when people still knocked on the door of the farmhouse to buy fresh eggs and potatoes from Spring Lane Farm. This was the shop in its infancy, which developed from selling produce at the top of the drive, to the establishment of the farm's own butchery in renovated calving sheds, to the introduction of a bakery where surplus beef was made into delicious pies, and then to a full refurbishment ten years later, which has brought all three elements under one roof, and provided a modern space to continue feeding demand for the top-quality and good value produce that Spring Lane Farm Shop has come to guarantee over the years.

Amongst this produce are the farm's home-grown potatoes and an amazing 18 varieties of sausage, all made in the butchery and sold in the shop. Where possible, everything is locally sourced, such as the carrots which hail from a local farm. The staff only travel a little farther, coming from the surrounding towns and villages with other members of the family in tow in some cases. Bakery manager Tammy is the sister of Jess, of Scotch egg fame, and all members of the Spencer family are still very actively involved.

Herbert Spencer bought the farm in the 1930s, and it has belonged to the Spencer family ever since. Because of this, customers know the family and the longstanding staff members well and have a lot of loyalty to the place – customers have been coming to the farm shop for more than three decades. One lady reminded them recently that she was the very first customer to come to the brand new butchery counter when it first opened, and she still puts in one of the farm shop's biggest orders at Christmas time as well as visiting two or three times a week year-round.

Spring Lane Farm Shop has certainly been a team effort, right down to the family getting stuck in when it came to building work, ready for the grand reopening in August 2017. Strong local ties and a (literally) down-to-earth outlook clearly work very well for the cheery lot at Spring Lane – and with a new era of growth ushered in through the recent renovation, everyone's got a spring in their step.

Spring Lane Farm Shop

Spring Lane Farm Shop
SCOTCH EGG

Jess, who makes these hand-moulded Scotch eggs at Spring Lane Farm Shop, has a reputation for being very particular when it comes to shaping them! If you can achieve the same beautifully spherical result at home, you'll be well on your way to impressing family and friends with these tasty traditional treats.

Preparation time: 5 minutes | Cooking time: 40 minutes | Serves 1-2

Ingredients

1 large free-range egg, hard-boiled

227g pork sausage meat

Fresh breadcrumbs

Method

Remove the shell from the hard-boiled egg, rinse with cold water and pat dry.

Flatten the sausage meat into the palm of your hand, making a slight well in the centre. Place the egg in the well and mould the sausage meat around the egg into a spherical shape. If needed, use a little water to smooth the outside of the sausage meat. This also helps the breadcrumbs to stick. Roll the ball in the breadcrumbs, ensuring all of the sausage meat is covered. Reshape if needed after coating in breadcrumbs.

Place the egg on a baking tray and bake for 40 minutes at 190°c until the sausage meat is cooked and the Scotch egg is golden brown. Leave to cool before serving.

The apple of HIS EYE

Starkey's Fruit are the proud owners of the only commercial orchard of 'the original' Bramley apples, and Suzannah Starkey has brought this 200-year heritage into the 21st century with her development and modernisation of the business.

The picturesque estate of Norwood Park lies just outside Southwell, and has been home to the Starkey family for over a century. The estate kitchen garden is now a busy fruit farm, especially at apple harvest time, and the Starkey signature variety is the Bramley Apple, thanks to Mary-Ann Brailsford who in 1809 planted a pip in her back garden in Southwell. Against the odds, this pip miraculously grew into a fruiting tree – edible apples usually only grow from grafted root stock – and thus the Bramley Seedling from Southwell became famous the world over.

In 1910, the first John Starkey planted a Bramley orchard at Norwood Park, and since then Starkey's Fruit has developed the only commercial orchard of original Bramleys. Sir John and a team of scientists from the University of Nottingham took a leaf culture, and after 15 years of trial and error created an exact genetic copy of the original Bramley seedling, conserving the unique character of this well-loved cooking apple for future generations. Along the way, they made the extraordinary discovery that like the original tree, Sir John's clones did not need sugar to sweeten the resulting fruit.

The Bramley apple is not generally known as a juicing apple, but Sir John started making farm-pressed bottled juice and compote from his apples, which had natural sweetness. Four years ago, John's daughter Suzannah joined the family business, and proceeded to modernise the production of all things Bramley. Starkey's Fruit now sell fresh apples as well as making and selling juices and compotes to a range of outlets, from large supermarkets to small local shops and greengrocers, including Fred Hallam of Beeston.

There are exciting developments ahead for the innovative family – look out for Bramley cider in the near future, which we certainly can't wait to taste! Last year, Suzannah won the Rural Business Award Innovation of the Year for producing Bramley apple juice pouches for Nottinghamshire County Council Schools, and was runner up in the Food & Drink Category for 'Passionately Promoting the Bramley'. Starkey's Fruit are also regular front runners at the Bramley Apple Festival in Southwell Minster, held at the end of October each year – a fitting spot for the champions of this local product with its fascinating history and, more importantly, great taste!

Starkey's Fruit
EXTRAORDINARY PORK
WITH STARKEY BRAMLEYS

Suzannah's background as a chef helped her to develop this dish, which she showcased to an important team of apple buyers when they visited the house and farm. Bramley apples are very versatile; however Suzannah has chosen to celebrate the traditional marriage of pork and apple.

Preparation time: approx. 3 hours, plus chilling overnight | Cooking time: approx. 7 hours | Serves 6

Ingredients

12 pig cheeks

1 onion

1 garlic bulb

250ml Starkey's Bramley Apple Juice

200g black pudding

350g Starkey's Bramley Compote

1g agar agar

Few drops green and red food colouring

100g flour

2 eggs, beaten

200g breadcrumbs

150ml cream

500g pork tenderloin

125g pancetta

Micro herbs, to garnish

Method

First, seal the pig cheeks in a pan over a medium-high heat, then place them in a pot with the garlic and onion. Add a generous splash of apple juice and cook in the oven at 100°c for 3-5 hours. Keeping the juice, shred the pork and press it into a block. Wrap in cling film and refrigerate overnight.

Next, prepare the accompaniments. To make a black pudding crumb, crumble up good quality black pudding and dry out at around 80°c for 90 minutes. To make Bramley apple balls, fill 24 half sphere moulds with the compote and place in the freezer. When frozen, pop out the half spheres, press together to make 12 spheres in total and push a cocktail stick into each one, then refreeze.

Now make an apple jelly by bringing the agar agar and 100ml of apple juice to the boil. Whisk thoroughly and remove from the heat, then add a few drops of green food colouring. Divide the jelly between two bowls and add a few drops of red food colouring to one of the bowls, but don't stir too thoroughly. Take the apple compote balls out of the freezer and dip each one first into the green jelly, and then into the speckled reddish jelly, to get the effect of the Starkey Bramley 'blush'. Carefully place the jelly coated balls onto a baking tray and freeze again. Bring them out an hour before serving.

To make the sauce, skim the fat off the leftover cooking juices from the pig cheeks and reduce down, then add a splash of cream and reduce again until a good consistency is achieved.

To assemble the dish, trim the pork tenderloin, taking off any sinews. Lay strips of pancetta on cling film and place the tenderloin across the strips so it can be rolled up tightly. Poach the wrapped tenderloin in apple juice for 20 minutes at 150°c. Use a meat thermometer to check when the centre of the tenderloin reaches 60°c. To get a crispy finish, pan fry the tenderloin whole and check again with the meat thermometer – it should reach 70°c.

Slice the chilled pulled pork into six portions and dip each into flour, beaten egg, then breadcrumbs. Shallow fry each piece until golden and crispy.

To serve

Suzannah recommends using a flat white plate to make all the components really stand out. Place two of the braised cheeks onto the plate, and scatter over black pudding crumbs. Cut the pork loin into 6 pieces at angles, and stand one piece up on the plate. Add two Bramley balls, then drizzle over some of the sauce. Garnish with micro herbs to finish.

Keeping it in
THE FAMILY

Thaymar's luxury ice creams and sorbets are sold all over the UK, but the place that started it all also boasts a farm shop and tea room – don't miss this trio of culinary treats tucked away in the Nottinghamshire countryside.

Thaymar Ice Cream began back in the 1980s when Thelma and Martin Cheetham devised a tasty and profitable way to use up surplus milk from their dairy herd. Today, their children Emily and Thomas have pivotal roles in the day-to-day management of the business as a whole, along with Emily's husband Tom Woodcock, who heads up production. It would be remiss not to mention the contribution of Tom and Emily's own children too, who earned their pocket money at Thaymar's temporary picking station, gathering produce for the Belvoir cordial that flavours Thaymar's well-loved Elderflower and Gooseberry ice cream.

As you might imagine, they are a close knit team, though it's not just family who stick around – Zoe White joined Thaymar as a waitress whilst still at school, and is now the office manager. Customers are very much part of the clan at Thaymar too – some regulars visit every single day, which we reckon is almost a better endorsement than the multiple Great Taste awards the ice cream has picked up over the years. The business doesn't need to spend much time on advertising, as the reputation of the ice cream and the tea room travels mostly by word of mouth, but the team certainly don't take that for granted.

They make a point of rewarding the effort their customers make to find them off the beaten track, by changing the tea room specials weekly, introducing brand new creations – the brilliant concept of a 'Yorkshire burrito' filled with slow-cooked beef brisket and roasted veg with chips on the side was a particular hit – and hosting off-the-cuff events such as murder mystery nights and gourmet dining experiences.

Expertly combining a very local and a nationwide appeal, Thaymar recently diversified into raising beef shorthorn and Hampshire Down sheep, which are butchered locally and brought back to head chef Jamie Manning, who has to get inventive in order to make use of every cut. Although Thaymar Ice Cream no longer has its own dairy herd – in a happy coincidence, the milk for all ice cream production is now sourced from a farm 5 miles down the road run by Tom's cousins – it still makes everything on site. This includes bespoke flavours developed to order, such as a mince pie ice cream for a pub planning their Christmas menu, and the 'Jess & John' ice cream – an espresso salted caramel flavour created for the eponymous couple's wedding day.

With so many facets to the business, what unites Thaymar's talents is an ethos that Emily puts very simply: 'whatever we do, it's got to be the best'. Whether they're serving sorbet, sirloin steak or a Sunday roast, this family business seems to have passed down the secret formula to success!

Thaymar Ice Cream

Thaymar Ice Cream
BBQ PULLED PORK

If the tea room ever takes this dish off the menu, the uproar from customers quickly returns it to pride of place! We are always being asked for the recipe, so now everyone can enjoy this absolute favourite at home too.

Preparation time: 15 minutes, plus 24 hours marinating | Cooking time: approx. 4 hours | Serves 4-6

Ingredients

1.3 kg pork shoulder, rind removed and remaining fat scored

For the spice rub:

1 tsp salt

1 tbsp smoked paprika

1 tbsp cumin

1 tsp black pepper

1 tbsp honey

1 tsp vegetable oil

For the BBQ sauce:

1 red onion

3 garlic cloves

2 tbsp vegetable oil

1 tsp cumin

3 tsp smoked paprika

70g tomato purée

600g tinned tomatoes

500ml beef stock

660ml cola

4 tbsp liquid smoke

Salt and pepper

Method

Mix all of the dry ingredients for the spice rub together and massage into the pork along with the honey and vegetable oil. Leave the pork to marinate up to 24 hours.

Preheat the oven to 200°c. Place the pork on a baking tray and into the oven, then after 25 minutes reduce the temperature to 140°c and leave the pork to cook for another hour.

Meanwhile, start to make the sauce. Slice the onions and garlic, then sauté in the vegetable oil for 5-10 minutes over a medium heat until they are soft and lightly coloured. Add the cumin and smoked paprika and continue to cook for 2 minutes. Stir in the tomato purée, tinned tomatoes, beef stock, cola and liquid smoke and continue to cook for a further 25 minutes, stirring occasionally. Blend into a smooth purée and season with salt and pepper to taste.

After the pork has had an hour in the oven at 140°c, pour the sauce over the pork and cover with foil. Return to the oven at the same temperature for a further 2 hours, occasionally basting the pork with the sauce. For the last 30 minutes, remove the foil to allow the sauce to reduce to a sticky consistency. Once cooked, the pork should be lovely and tender and can be pulled apart with two forks and mixed into the sticky sauce.

To serve

We suggest loading the pulled pork onto warm bread with homemade coleslaw.

Thaymar Ice Cream
CHOCOLATE ORANGE BREAD AND BUTTER PUDDING

Similarly to their pulled pork, the tea room staff are under strict orders from devoted customers to keep Emily's Christmas leftovers-inspired pudding on the menu at all times. Strangely enough, until she included 'chocolate orange' in the name, it hadn't sold at all – thank goodness people came to their senses, as we wouldn't want anyone to miss out on the chance to make this at home.

Preparation time: 15 minutes | Cooking time: 40 minutes | Serves 4

Ingredients

750g Italian panettone (or other fruity bread)

125g dark chocolate, broken into chunks

125g butter

400ml cream

300ml orange juice

3 oranges, zested

5 eggs

100g sugar

Sprinkle of Demerara sugar

Chocolate curls

Method

Slice the panettone and layer the slices into a 22 x 28cm ovenproof dish, tucking chunks of chocolate into the layers between slices. In a small saucepan, gently melt the butter and cream until all the butter has melted. Make sure the mixture does not boil. Remove from the heat and add the orange juice and orange zest to the cream mixture.

In a separate bowl, whisk the eggs and sugar, then gradually add the cream mixture whilst whisking to get a nice smooth custard. Pour over the panettone slices, allowing the custard to soak through all of the layers. If time allows, refrigerate the pudding for 30 minutes as this will help the panettone soak up all the liquid.

Bake at 160°c for approximately 25 minutes until golden brown and set. Let it cool slightly, then sprinkle with Demerara sugar and chocolate curls.

To serve

We suggest serving a big slice of the warm, oozy pudding with Thaymar Brandy and Orange ice cream. Can you blame us?

Time
FOR TEA

Owners Jo Bounds and Diane Elliott shared a vision of providing all the welcoming traditions of a great British afternoon tea when they opened Tiffin Tea House back in 2011. The result is a timeless place for customers of all ages to enjoy home-cooked meals and slices of freshly baked cake. All washed down, of course, with a pot of proper loose leaf tea...

In the six years since its opening, Tiffin has established itself as a firm favourite within Nottingham, and for good reason. The pretty and welcoming interior, along with the inviting aroma of homemade goods, are just part of the charm, as the tight-knit team provide some of the city's friendliest service in a venue at the heart of its community. It's a formula so winning that Jo and Diane have recently had to expand Tiffin's premises, taking over neighbouring community venture Renew 37's space on Fridays, Saturdays and Sundays to create a bigger tea party for everyone!

Tiffin frequently welcomes guests wanting to celebrate everything from birthdays to baby showers, christenings and hen dos. Alongside these popular events, they've also launched a bi-monthly evening restaurant, featuring a three-course Mediterranean-inspired menu – one of West Bridgford's first BYOB pop-ups.

It's safe to say the Tiffin team aren't afraid of a challenge; in 2016 they were chosen to cater for an event attended by Team GB's regional Olympic medal winners. The tea house is also a popular location for visiting film crews, which have included Come Dine With Me, Don't Tell The Bride and Location, Location, Location.

For Tiffin's loyal customers, the appeal lies in the tea house's delicious and honest food, its 'think local' mind set, its door-always-open approach to service and, of course, the cakes. Inventive flavours, showcased in the Cake of the Month, have included everything from pumpkin to peanut butter, and Tiffin is equally happy to cater for gluten-free guests with an impressively wide range of offerings to suit all tastes. The cherry on top of this particularly perfect cake is Tiffin's unrivalled range of international teas, uniting the more traditional aspects of a time-honoured tea house with a modern, forward-thinking, community venue. We'll drink to that!

Tiffin Tea House
LIME & COCONUT CAKE

This tropical cake is a popular feature of the Tiffin Tea House counter, created by owners Jo and Diane who turn out up to 22 delicious bakes every day! Follow their icing instructions carefully to reproduce the striking finish on this 3-layered delight.

Preparation time: 30 minutes | Cooking time: approx. 20 minutes | Serves 8

Ingredients

For the sponge:

250g margarine (Stork is our preference)

250g caster sugar

5 eggs

1 lime, zested

25g unsweetened desiccated coconut

250g self-raising flour

For the filling:

100g pure creamed coconut

250g coconut oil

400g icing sugar

50ml milk (or water, if you prefer)

150g lime marmalade

For the icing and decoration:

1 lime, juiced

Icing sugar

40g desiccated coconut

Green food colouring

Method

Before beginning, ensure all the ingredients are at room temperature, and preheat the oven to 180°c (160°c for a fan oven). Grease and line three 20cm (8") round cake tins.

To make the sponge, cream the margarine and caster sugar until the mixture is light in colour. Gradually add the eggs, mixing thoroughly, then stir in the lime zest and coconut. Sift the flour and fold it in carefully to create an airy texture.

Divide the sponge mixture between the three tins and bake in the preheated oven for approximately 20 minutes. Once cooked, leave the cakes in the tins to cool slightly, then remove them from the tins to cool completely.

To make the coconut cream, warm the creamed coconut and then beat it with the coconut oil until they are combined and the mixture is soft. Add half of the icing sugar and all the milk or water, mix thoroughly and then add the remaining icing sugar.

Next, make up the glacé icing using the lime juice and enough icing sugar for a smooth, but not too runny consistency. In a separate bowl, gradually add green food colouring to the desiccated coconut and keep mixing with a fork until all the pieces are the desired colour.

Set aside approximately one third of the coconut cream for the sides and piping, and layer the three cakes with coconut cream and lime marmalade. Once the sponges are firmly in place, evenly coat the sides with the remaining coconut cream. Place the green desiccated coconut on a plate and carefully roll the sides of the cake in the coconut. Fill an icing bag with the last of the coconut cream and pipe stars around the top edge of the cake (we use a number eight piping tube for this) to form a barrier all the way round. Finally, flood the top of the cake with the lime glacé icing and finish with an extra sprinkling of green coconut pieces.

Tipple, tea,
OR BOTH?

Tipsy T offers what its name suggests – a comfortable bar to relax in with an impressive range of drinks, as well as a daytime café serving traditional English food with teas and coffees – in the increasingly popular Mapperley Top area.

Owner and creator Chris envisaged a local, independent café bar for her fellow Mapperley residents where people could relax in a comfortable atmosphere, enjoying both a daytime bite to eat and an evening out, without having to go right into the city centre for either. By combining her own love of gin with this idea, Chris has created something quite unique at Tipsy T. Easy to find, hard to leave, impossible to forget – the café bar has lived up to its maxim and seen regular custom since the opening in July 2016.

During the daylight hours, there's a lovely traditional feel to the food menu – classics such as ploughman's lunch, pork pies and toasted teacakes embrace the Englishness of the Tipsy T concept. There's a host of breakfast options for early birds, accompanied by coffee from 200 Degrees, which we can certainly recommend! You can also, of course, have your very own Tipsy T – an afternoon tea of delicious sandwiches and cakes, accompanied by a cocktail of your choice. Weekends allow even more time to relax there, with lazy Sunday afternoon's featuring live music, and a beer garden for sunny days.

Even when the sun's going down and other cafés are closing their doors, Tipsy T welcomes its customers to stay around as it transforms into a relaxed evening destination, the main attraction of which has to be its incredibly well-stocked bar. Alongside beers, spirits and cocktail components, it boasts a range of over 150 gins, including regional gins such as Two Birds from Leicestershire, Sir Robin of Locksley from Sheffield and of course Nottingham's very own Redsmiths. The selection is added to as and when Chris discovers a promising new gin, or is approached by small distillers such as Pin Gin from Louth.

To help customers narrow down their choices, Chris features a Gin of the Week – always a popular seller, as it's likely to be something people haven't tried before. There are also monthly gin tasting events at Tipsy T for anyone looking to expand their horizons or just have a bit of fun; customers who come back for the next one (and the next one, and the next…) show that it's a great evening out. Whether you visit for the café, the bar, or an event, the friendly Tipsy T team are keen to make sure it's a great experience – and surely an unmissable one for gin lovers – that's diverse enough for everyone to enjoy, day or night!

Tipsy T
ROSE GARDEN

This is a deliciously sweet summer cocktail starring one of our favourite gins – Larios Rosa. It's a strawberry and cucumber infusion with a subtle hint of elderflower. Much like a Mojito, this is a built drink, negating the need for expensive equipment like a Boston Shaker or Manhattan strainer.

Preparation time: 5-10 minutes | Serves 1

Ingredients

4 cucumber slices

15ml elderflower cordial

50ml Larios Rosa gin

125ml Fentimans Rose Lemonade

1 strawberry, to garnish

1 cucumber slice, to garnish

Crushed ice

Method

Using a muddling stick (or similar), crush 4 slices of cucumber in a tall glass, add some crushed ice and pour in 15ml elderflower cordial, followed by 50ml of Larios Rosa gin. Stir gently until the mix turns pale green. Fill the glass with more crushed ice and top with 125ml of Fentimans Rose Lemonade. Garnish the rim of the glass with strawberry, cucumber and/or mint leaves and serve.

Tipsy T
MURDER ON THE ORIENT ESPRESSO

A twist on the classic Espresso Martini, this drink includes salted caramel and plenty of caramelised brown sugar to balance the bitterness of the espresso. We use locally roasted coffee from 200 Degrees and Two Birds Salted Caramel Vodka from Leicestershire.

Preparation time: 5-10 minutes | Serves 1

Ingredients

1 shot of espresso coffee (alternatively, use 15ml strong French press coffee)

25ml Two Birds Salted Caramel English Vodka

25ml Tia Maria

15ml Monin caramel syrup

Fine Demerara sugar

3 coffee beans, to garnish

Method

Brew the espresso and pour it over ice into a Boston Shaker. Add 25ml Two Birds Salted Caramel Vodka, 25ml Tia Maria and 15ml Monin Caramel Syrup. Shake well until ice cold. Strain into a martini glass, ensuring a creamy light brown foam forms on the drink. Sprinkle fine Demerara sugar onto the surface and caramelise with a blowtorch. Garnish with three whole coffee beans.

Everything
ON TOAST

A family-run business that combines a relaxed place to eat and drink with a deli and gift shop, championing local produce and great homemade food.

Opening Toast was a real leap of faith for owners Sharon and Clare, since they had little experience in hospitality and had both previously worked in education when their joint venture started life two years ago. They have since created a perfect spot for a range of customers to unwind, meet friends, study and of course enjoy some of Nottinghamshire's best produce from amazing local suppliers, both to buy and to sample in the delicious menu.

Toast is one of the few local stockists of Stokes of Lincoln coffee, and is supplied by Nottingham-based Lee & Fletcher for the extensive range of teas. Freshly baked cake by Simply Cakes is an ideal accompaniment to your hot drink, or you could satisfy your sweet tooth with a doughnut, courtesy of Doughnotts, on weekends. Johnny Pusztai is a regular visitor at Toast, either for a meal and a natter or to deliver all of Toast's meat products such as smoked bacon, Lincolnshire sausage, ham and pastrami. Welbeck Bakehouse's sourdough bread is the perfect partner for these, delivered daily along with a range of irresistible pastries.

To wash it all down, there are soft drinks and ales from local supplier Harry & Parker – being a licenced premises, Toast serve wine, prosecco and beers which no doubt go down very well at the bookable afternoon events such as baby showers and afternoon teas for a special celebration on Sunday afternoons. With the unhurried, friendly atmosphere Sharon and Clare have cultivated, it's not surprising that these are popular and get great reviews. Their customers represent a mix of residents, students, professionals, families and four-legged friends, so anybody feels welcome.

The staff are a mixture of backgrounds and ages too, but Toast has created a real family atmosphere in the café and deli. For Sharon and Clare, it's important to ensure that newcomers fit in well with the team and are happy in their work, more so than having the right skills. On Saturdays the whole family really does pitch in too, with the owners' husbands and daughters as well as Clare's daughter-in-law coming in to help out.

Open seven days a week, there is nothing quite like Toast in the immediate area. From the freshly made food in the café to the outlet for local arts and crafts, the café and deli really is a one-stop wonder for incredible Nottinghamshire produce. Sauce Shop, Freshly Spiced, Black Acres soap and candles, jewellery by Sam at LillyAlexandra and handmade cards from Chris Hicklin are just a few names to look out for, but we recommend a visit to explore and enjoy everything on offer at Toast for yourself!

Millionaires
Shortbread
£2.50

Rocky
Road
£2.50

TOAST

TOAST

TOAST

OPEN

Toast
THREE BEAN SOUP WITH CHORIZO

Our three bean soup with chorizo is one of our current shop specials, and very popular with our lunchtime customers who want a hearty, tasty meal. We use only the best chorizo, made locally by our award-winning butcher, Johnny Pusztai at JT Beedham & Sons. It has a great, authentic taste and both cooks and presents beautifully.

Preparation time: 10 minutes | Cooking time: approx. 1 hour | Serves 6

Ingredients

1 garlic bulb

½ link (approx. 100g) of chorizo

1 tbsp olive oil

1 tsp chilli flakes

1 bunch fresh coriander

1 tsp cumin seeds

1 tbsp smoked paprika

2 sticks celery, chopped

2 spring onions, chopped

4 medium-sized fresh tomatoes, roughly chopped

400g tin tomatoes

500g carton passata

2 x 410g tins haricot beans (if you can't easily get these substitute 2 tins of baked beans)

2 x 420g tins kidney beans

2 x 240g tins butter beans

Method

Chop the bottom off the garlic bulb and remove the stem and any papery outer shell but leave the skins on the individual cloves. Set aside. Slice the chorizo into two pieces; roughly chop one half into small chunks and slice the other half into rounds.

Heat the olive oil in a heavy-based pan, and gently fry the sliced chorizo. Remove chorizo from pan, put to one side and without cleaning the pan, fry the chilli flakes, half of the coriander, cumin seeds and paprika. Stir until the spices are sizzling, then add the prepared garlic bulb, celery, spring onion and fresh tomatoes to the pan. Reduce the heat, and gently fry until soft.

Add half of the tinned tomatoes and all the passata to the vegetables, and bring the mixture to the boil. Remove the pan from the heat and, using a stick blender, carefully blitz until the soup base is smooth.

Drain the haricot, butter and kidney beans and add them all to the soup base. Add the cooked sliced chorizo along with the other half of the tinned tomatoes, and simmer the soup for 30 minutes.

5 minutes before the simmering time is up, chop the remaining coriander and stir in gently. Add salt and pepper to taste.

To serve

Fry the remaining roughly chopped chorizo. Ladle the soup into bowls and add a swirl of sour cream to the top. Scatter the fried chunks of chorizo on top of the soup, and serve with chunky bread – we use Welbeck Bakehouse Deli Rye, with caraway seeds.

A perfect winter warmer!

All under ONE ROOF

Packed to the rafters with fresh produce, friendly cafés, treasure troves of homeware, hardware and craft supplies along with welcoming traders and stallholders, Victoria Market is a Nottingham institution with a deservedly long history.

Victoria Market is the only indoor market in Nottingham, and has existed in the Victoria Centre since 1972, when the mall was purpose-built to house greater shopping opportunities for the city. The history of the market itself in Nottingham, however, stretches even further back.

William Peveril, builder of Nottingham Castle, founded a market on neutral ground for the two boroughs of 11th century Nottingham, in a space that became the Old Market Square. It was an enormous market by today's standards – five and a half acres of stalls, traders and shoppers – and functioned from the 11th century until 1928. Following this, a central market existed in Nottingham from the 1920s, until it moved in the 1970s to its new and current home.

Markets have always been places of great importance to the community, as evidenced by Nottingham's long history of these important social spaces, and Victoria Market is keeping that tradition alive by offering a really diverse and welcoming mix of trade.

The sellers are local people, many of them running family businesses or longstanding enough to have seen 30 plus years of trade. From fishmongers and butchers to florists and haberdashers, it's the ideal place to shop if you're looking for a bargain on quality produce.

Having more than one greengrocer in the market, for example, means that shoppers can pick and choose the fruit and vegetables they deem the best value, and it's possible to get everything on that shopping list ticked off without having to trail round lots of different shops across the city.

Whether it's flowers and plants, beauty products, crafts and fabrics, jewellery, electronics or perhaps a single nut and bolt (which can be picked up at the aptly-named Aladdin's Cave, a real treasure trove selling anything and everything you can think of for your home and hardware needs) you're after, Victoria Market has got you covered.

And of course, buying from traders is a much more personable experience, especially from those as well-established as the Victoria Market group – some of whom, like Stones family-run stall, were originally part of the central market, and moved with it into the Victoria Centre.

Some of the most popular food stalls are rooted deeply in tradition too – but not just English traditions. Jamaican cuisine has proved a hit with locals, expertly cooked by proprietors Trevor and Yolandi at TY's Continental, whose curried mutton and jerk dishes are not to be missed. If you need an antidote to all that spice afterwards, Federici is a family-run ice cream parlour, selling real Italian gelato to the lucky public at Victoria Market.

Victoria Market is home to a local culinary institution in The Nottingham Mushy Pea Stall. Mushy peas are a real favourite – and you might almost say delicacy – around these parts, the stall also sells faggots made by local butchers Bonds, and is rarely without a hungry customer or two.

For those not wanting to eat on the go, there are also four restaurants and cafés in the market, equally as popular as the food stalls judging by the regulars, some of whom will head straight for their favourite seats as soon as the shutters come up.

In 2012, the Food Hall in Victoria Market was refurbished by the council – who own the market and act as landlords for all the traders there – to increase the space available for food stalls. It's now an attractive and modernised section of the market, and with more traders offering Halal products than before, it reflects the market's ethos of inclusivity too.

It's not just the people of Nottingham who have recognised the quality of Victoria Market – in 2008 it won the award for the Greenest Market in the Midlands, from the National Market Traders Federation, and has a reputation for the quality of its fresh produce which has lasted throughout its years of operation.

Victoria Market is open to the public from 9am until 5pm every day except Sundays, and is easy to travel to by car, tram or bus. It's a special place for many from all walks of life, and aims to provide for everyone who visits – from students on a tight budget, to retirees with time to enjoy the social aspect, busy families and people of all backgrounds – with a friendly welcome.

This longstanding Nottingham gem certainly seems set to continue its thoughtful balancing of traditional market values with the needs of today's traders and shoppers, and remains a great place to meet and socialise, as well as one of the best spots to shop savvy in Nottingham.

Eyes on THE PIE

Vork Pie is the brainchild of Sophie Neill, a producer of 100% vegan pies based in Nottingham who is single-handedly making sure nobody misses out on one of Britain's best comfort food inventions...

In 2014 Sophie Neill decided that the time had come to strike out on her own, and began brainstorming ideas for a new business in the food world, which would develop into the pie-eyed kitchen in the not too distant future. Inspired by the very traditional London pie and mash shops on a visit to the capital, but having been a vegetarian since the age of 16, Sophie realised that there could be a way to marry up her love of drinking real ale in great pubs with the bar snacks that were so often disappointingly limited for non-meat eaters. She enrolled on one of The School of Artisan Food's short courses and learned everything there is to know about making pie pastry, and from there developed her own vegetarian hot water crust recipe.

Having taste-tested her creations in a mate's pub, The Johnson Arms, Sophie began to develop vegan recipes, including a new pastry, from her vegetarian beginnings and found them to be equally as successful with hungry customers. Vork Pie is now completely vegan, as is Sophie, and her current pie options include 'The Traditional' – herby and savoury enough to satisfy even the most dedicated pork pie fan – butternut squash spiced with cumin and ginger, and piri piri, which is also the flavour of one of two vegan Scotch eggs Sophie has created.

As well as being in pride of place on The Johnson Arms' Sunday dinner menu, you can find Vork Pie products at Debbie Bryan, The Peacock, Sneinton vegan market and also at The V Spot vegan store in Sherwood to name a few; as well as at local farmers' markets and vegan events up and down the country. Even Melton Mowbray, the pork pie capital of the UK, offered up a Bronze medal to Vork's tamarind sweet potato pie at the 2016 British Pie Awards, in the vegetarian category no less (there isn't a vegan one yet) up against competition from various cheesy fillings – a hard act to follow in Nottinghamshire especially!

Having started life in the kitchen of her first pub stockist, she moved from there to her home kitchen, but outgrew that quickly, and then bought an industrial unit to refit for catering. Vork Pie is growing in size and reputation. Sophie now has an apprentice pie-maker working alongside her, and is seeing repeat custom from pie enthusiasts, vegan or otherwise, at many of the markets she visits. Her next step is readying the business for an online sales presence, and of course there are always new ideas to develop, inspired by the great feedback Sophie gets at events, which drives her forward and enables her to keep producing her delicious handmade, hand-crimped, very special Vork creations.

Vork Pie
AUBERGINE PARMIGIANA PIE

A rich, comforting, Italian-inspired pie topped with sweet potato. This recipe is designed to be made in individual pie dishes, making it easy to freeze for a really quick weeknight dinner. Like all of Vork Pie's products, this pie is suitable for vegans, and extremely tasty!

Preparation time: 15 minutes | Cooking time: approx. 1 ½ hours | Serves 4

Ingredients

1 large or 2 small aubergines, sliced into 1 cm thick rounds

1 tbsp olive oil

1 small red onion, finely diced

2-3 garlic cloves, crushed

Salt and pepper, to taste

3 beef tomatoes, chopped

1 tsp dried basil

1 tsp dried oregano

125ml vegan red wine

8 green olives, sliced

1 x 225g tin of green lentils, drained

12 sundried tomatoes, finely chopped

2 medium sweet potatoes, peeled and diced

Dash of plant-based milk (soya, oat, almond etc.)

Method

Using a large frying pan, fry the aubergine slices in the olive oil until they are soft and browned, without crowding the pan. Set aside to drain on kitchen paper. Next, boil or steam the sweet potatoes until soft (around 10-14 minutes) and set aside. Using the same pan as you used for the aubergine, fry onion and garlic in olive oil until soft, then add the chopped beef tomatoes, basil and oregano and season with salt and black pepper to taste. Stir in the sun-dried tomatoes, add the wine and simmer until the sauce thickens.

Next, add the olives and green lentils, heat for a further 5 minutes and preheat the oven to 180°c (160°c fan). In small individual round pie dishes, layer up the pie filling like you would a lasagne, starting with a tablespoon of the tomato mixture, then a slice of aubergine. Repeat this twice more and finish with a layer of aubergine. Mash the sweet potato, seasoning with salt and pepper and adding a little plant-based milk, divide into four portions and top each pie with the mash, using a fork or teaspoon make a pattern on the top.

Bake the pies in the preheated oven for 25-30 minutes, and enjoy as a hearty meal with vegetables of your choice on the side.

Artisan food AND DRINK

The Welbeck Estate is the place to visit, learn, work and live in the heart of Sherwood Forest.

Hidden away in the lush Nottinghamshire countryside between Worksop and Mansfield, Welbeck offers a truly inspiring environment for those working, living or just visiting the traditional landed estate. This beautiful location is home to a thriving artisan food community, five businesses from which are featured in the pages of this chapter. Ottar Chocolate, The School of Artisan Food, The Welbeck Bakehouse, Welbeck Abbey Brewery and Welbeck Farm Shop produce some of the finest delicacies in the area, and are all award winners in their fields.

The producers at Welbeck are all connected by a common ethos of sustainability, innovation and diversification as well as by their collaborations and, of course, a drive to create excellence in all the food and drink they produce. Alison Swan-Parente founded The Welbeck Bakehouse on recognising that the Dukeries – the area of North Nottinghamshire within which the estate stretches over its 15,000 acres, named after the four historic neighbouring Ducal estates – lacked a great bread-making culture, and was keen to fill the gap with a skilled and passionate enterprise. The School of Artisan Food followed a year later, providing an ideal environment for the bakers, and anyone else interested in artisanal food production to perfect their skills. Welbeck Abbey Brewery was set up as part of a regeneration of the estate in the renovated outbuildings that

Ottar Chocolate has also made its home in. Located in The Courtyard, Welbeck Farm Shop is the longest-established of the five and proudly stocks all of the products made on the estate.

Welbeck is still a working estate, with a deer park, ancient woodlands, lakes and grazing pastures alongside the historic village. Having started life as a Premonstratensian Abbey in 1153, to then become a Cavalier residence in the 17th century, and later an Edwardian palace, the range of Welbeck's heritage is astonishing, and proudly preserved by the residents and business owners working there today.

Three of the five featured businesses have offered customers the chance to recreate some of the dishes they develop and serve at the estate, and all of the products from The Welbeck Bakehouse, Welbeck Abbey Brewery and Ottar Chocolate are stocked in the farm shop amongst many other highlights. Whether you're picking up fantastic ingredients to use at home, want a day out in beautiful surroundings or are interested in the history of the estate, we highly recommend a visit to The Courtyard at Welbeck to sample all the delights of this unique and food-focused haven.

Chocolate of THE FUTURE

Ottar Chocolate is an independent business situated on the beautiful Welbeck Estate, creating innovative award-winning real chocolate from natural, freshly made ingredients.

Shelly Preston was appointed creative director and head chocolatier at Ottar Chocolate in 2016, following six years of production on the Welbeck Estate. She describes Ottar as a very modern chocolate company, leaving old fashioned conceptions of what chocolate is and should be far behind, as well as upholding an important commitment to fair, ethical and sustainable chocolate making.

Ottar aims to create products based around what people really want to eat, so that they taste fresh and wonderful without losing any of the fun we associate with chocolate. Most importantly, Ottar ensures that the products are made with real chocolate, natural ingredients and an absolute dedication to vibrancy of flavour and quality in every aspect of the production process. The Ottar team passionately believe that real, quality chocolate shouldn't be a guilty treat, and should be just as available as more commercial industrially produced confectionery.

You might describe Ottar as a 'holistic chocolatier' – from beekeeping to cheese-making, the company adopts a very DIY approach to creating not just the chocolate itself, but all the fillings, sweet pastry and accoutrements that make each product so special. Jams, jellies, curds, peanut butters, caramel sauces, chocolate spread and fresh marshmallow (for the unmissable Marshmallow Teacakes) are all made in the Ottar kitchen, bringing delightful chocolates, confectionery and sweet pastry back to life in a grown-up and admirably particular fashion.

The flavours are botanically-inspired, reflecting the land the ingredients are sourced from, and many have earned impressive accolades despite Ottar's young age as a business. The blackcurrant, bay and Clementine ganache and the sweet sea salt fennel caramel are both Academy of Chocolate 2017 Gold Winners, closely followed by four other Silver and Bronze awards in this year alone. Ottar's chocolate partners are a crucial part of the story when it comes to producing excellence – Duffy's, Valrhona, Pump St Bakery and Akesson's all source the best raw ingredients in the best way, paying the right prices and importing beans directly from cacao farmers and small cooperatives so that everyone involved is justly rewarded.

You can buy Ottar Chocolate's products online from their website, or visit the concession in Welbeck Farm Shop whilst enjoying a day out in The Courtyard at Welbeck – whilst you're there, why not look into Shelly's chocolate-making course at The School of Artisan Food?

Ottar believes that everyone has the right to enjoy real chocolate, and that we should all invest chocolate that matters. This unique company's innovation, passion and dedication to the cause mean that Ottar chocolate is worth every bean.

Brewed to PERFECTION

Working from renovated outbuildings on the Welbeck Estate, the award-winning Welbeck Abbey Brewery creates real ale inspired by the history of its surroundings and its dedicated team members.

General Manager Claire Monk set up Welbeck Abbey Brewery in 2011 as part of the regeneration of the Welbeck Estate, which involved repurposing buildings as business venues for artisan producers. Having studied microbiology and biochemistry at university, Claire then learnt her trade at Kelham Island Brewery before being deemed the best person for the job at Welbeck, and now oversees a team of eight in the converted farm building that houses all the brewing equipment and office.

James Gladman took over the role of head brewer from Claire two years ago, and has already excelled in the position, creating several award-winning brews. The brewery also has an in-house graphic designer and marketing officer, Jess Low, who is responsible for designing the mini-kegs and pump clips for the monthly specials. She goes to impressive lengths to imbibe the brand with the history of Welbeck Estate, even contacting the on-site archivists to source an 18th century etching for the 'Greendale Oak' label design, amongst other buried treasures.

They're a fun-loving crew but serious when it comes to producing excellent beer, even down to tending the home-grown hop plant outside the office door which they hope to one day brew from. Welbeck Abbey Brewery produces roughly 15,000 pints per week and will generally have three or four beers fermenting at a time. There are six core beers in cask per month, as well as three specials to complete the line-up, which are always inspired by historic tales from the Welbeck Estate or dedicated to a member of the team.

Welbeck Abbey Brewery sticks with tried and tested tradition when it comes to brewing methods, never canning its ale and even hand-bottling a special edition which was aged in imported French red wine barrels and matured underneath the Abbey itself. The team are always on the lookout for new opportunities though, working with a different charity each year to develop a charitable ale, and creating speciality ales for the brewery's taps – such as Carlton Knight at the Grey Horses Inn in Carlton in Lindrick, which sits very well alongside the full range of Welbeck beer available there.

There are also plenty of online stockists and independent bottle shops where you can buy Welbeck Abbey Brewery beer, and as you might expect, the brewery has a close working relationship with other Welbeck businesses. Look out for the beer and cheese matching course at The School of Artisan Food, as well as products used at The Welbeck Bakehouse and Welbeck Farm Shop – the latter is always fully stocked and in the know when it comes to this very special Welbeck beer.

Real bakers,
BETTER BREAD

The Welbeck Bakehouse is an independent award-winning artisan-style bakery specialising in sourdough and Viennoiserie, in a secluded spot on the picturesque Welbeck Estate.

Firing up the ovens in 2008, The Welbeck Bakehouse built its foundations on a passion for creating and promoting 'Real Bread'. Avid supporters of The Real Bread Campaign, and inspired by their initial hunger to improve the day-to-day quality of nutrition, the team has seen the bakery grow at an impressive rate to supply an array of independent businesses throughout the local area.

If you think there are any hidden ingredients in the products, you would be mistaken! The Welbeck Bakehouse never adds artificial additives or improvers, and takes immense pride in producing a multitude of delicious baked goods using pre-ferments and slow fermentation methods. As a business it is passionate about sourcing locally and organically wherever possible. This even includes using produce from other businesses based on the Welbeck Estate, such as Stichelton cheese and ale from Welbeck Abbey Brewery, and also working closely with Ottar Chocolate.

The original sourdough culture has been nurtured since 2008, with the bakers using it to produce fresh bread daily, then 'refreshing' the culture which enhances flavour in the loaves and helps to naturally extend the shelf-life of the end product. Sourdough's health benefits are becoming more widely recognised, and are due to the process of long-fermentation, which renders the minerals in the dough more readily available for absorption by the body. As sourdough should only contain flour, salt, water, The Welbeck Bakehouse produces an extensive selection of vegan options too.

Emma Hall heads up the whole operation, overseeing the extremely hard-working and talented bakers, delivery drivers and administrative teams who all contribute to the seven-day-a-week business. This dedication to creating such high-quality products has united a bakery team from all walks of life, and all the bakers are extremely involved with each stage of the process, from hand-scaling each product to dreaming up new seasonal specialities.

Various accolades such as Highly Commended in Britain's Best Sourdough in 2017, Gold and Silver in the 2016 Tiptree Bread Awards and two prestigious Great Taste awards in 2016 celebrate the skill of the team, who are also passionate about celebrating artisan bread-making, working with local schools and charities through donations to food banks, talks and workshops, and engaging with the community.

As a wholesale bakery, The Welbeck Bakehouse delivers freshly baked products to a stream of businesses across the East Midlands and South Yorkshire. Pop into any of its suppliers (including Welbeck Farm Shop!) to grab yourself a treat, and allow your taste buds the chance to marvel at the unrivalled flavour of the humble sourdough loaf.

The Welbeck
Bakehouse

WELBECK

The Welbeck Bakehouse
LEMON AND POPPY SEED BRIOCHE SWIRLS

The bakers at The Welbeck Bakehouse developed this recipe as a seasonal product – an idea which not only celebrates seasonal flavours but also allows a chance to create something new! Showcasing the potential of brioche as a delicious sweet treat, rather than just a plain bun, head baker Jack Arkless recommends serving these with homemade lemon curd and clotted cream.

Preparation time: 30 minutes, plus 10-12 hours resting and 1-2 hours proofing
| Cooking time: 20 minutes | Serves 7

Ingredients

For the brioche:

500g type 00 flour

15g fresh yeast

7½g salt

200g whole eggs

100g milk

55g caster sugar

125g softened butter, cut into small cubes

1 lemon, zested and juiced

100g poppy seeds

For the icing:

500g icing sugar

1 tsp lemon juice

2 tsp cold water

Method

In a large bowl combine the whole eggs and milk, then add the flour, yeast and salt. Mix until the dough comes together, then knead for a further 15-20 minutes. If using an electric mixer, mix on a slow speed for 2-3 minutes using the dough hook attachment and then on a medium/fast speed for a further 6-8 minutes. At this point the dough should be soft, glossy and elastic.

Now add half the butter and half the sugar, mix for 4-5 minutes to incorporate both into the dough, and repeat. Remember to scrape down the side of the bowl periodically during both stages of adding the butter and sugar. Once you cannot see any lumps of butter, the dough is ready and will be a bit softer and more glossy and elastic than before. Place the dough into a large bowl that has been lightly greased, cover and place in the fridge for a minimum of 2 hours. The longer the dough is left at this stage, the better, so overnight is best. Resting the dough helps to develop the flavours and makes it much easier to work with.

Take the brioche dough out of the fridge and tip onto a lightly floured surface. Roll the dough out to form a rectangular shape about 4mm thick. Brush the dough with lemon juice and scatter over the lemon zest. Cover the rectangle with a thin layer of poppy seeds, then roll it tightly from the base of the rectangle all the way up until you have a brioche log resembling a Swiss roll. Cut the roll into slices of your desired thickness; we suggest 5cm. Place the rounds on a baking tray or in individual ramekins. At The Welbeck Bakehouse we use metal muffin rings to hold the shape of the rolls. Cover the whole tray with a plastic bag and leave to prove for 1-2 hours.

When your brioche buns have proved, bake for 15-20 minutes at 180°c. When they are done, remove from the oven and allow to cool, then mix together the icing sugar with the little bit of water and lemon juice until you have a thick but dropping consistency. Dip the top of your baked brioche bun into the glacé icing, stand upright and leave to set.

From field to FARM SHOP

Welbeck Farm Shop have been selling the freshest, highest quality produce at Welbeck for over a decade, focusing on low food miles and the rich heritage of the land around it.

The award-winning Welbeck Farm Shop sits at the heart of the artisanal food community found on the Welbeck Estate. Joe Parente, whose recipe is overleaf, is the founder and director, and the shop is managed by Oliver Stubbins. Together they continue to ensure that everything on the shelves or behind the counters is a product they are proud to sell, including of course the Made at Welbeck range, featuring Welbeck Abbey Brewery, Ottar Chocolate and The Welbeck Bakehouse amongst others. In fact, two thirds of the entire product range is sourced from or prepared at the historic estate, such as the raw milk delivered fresh from the dairy every morning.

With five Great Taste awards in 2017 alone, Welbeck Farm Shop has steadily gained a reputation as one of the country's best, and its cooperative relationship with the land is central to its success. The philosophy for sourcing products is 'start local' – evidenced by the venison and game larder, stocked with the results of shoots on the estate, and Welbeck's very own asparagus and pumpkins from this year's bountiful harvest. Seasonal produce and the presence of some very well-fed Welbeck pigs mean the farm shop is close to being a zero-waste business, as well as having very few food miles on the clock. Rhubarb Farm, a social enterprise five minutes down the road, is another great example of how Welbeck Farm

Shop really values the countryside and the local suppliers who also rely on it.

As well as stocking the best of their produce, Oliver and the team work closely with everyone who supplies the farm shop, and even ask for taste-testing volunteers (of which we bet there are many) from the estate. Many of the staff are also locals, and have worked at the farm shop for as many years as it's been open, meaning regular customers know them well and enjoy the kind of service, friendly interaction and knowledgeable guidance that you'd struggle to find in a supermarket. The shop relies mostly on word of mouth and repeat custom, enticing visitors in (and rightly so) with its display of curing and maturing pork and beef in the windows of the shop.

As the home of all the products created by our other featured Welbeck food and drink producers, Welbeck Farm Shop is a destination not to be missed on your visit to The Courtyard at Welbeck, where you can also browse in the two galleries and stop for a bite at the café. With its incredible range of products and the expertise of its staff, there's reason enough to make a special trip to Welbeck just for the shop though, as so many returning customers and delighted first-time visitors do seven days a week throughout the year.

STONE
k Goats Cheese
Herefordshire
8.99
4.50

Welbeck Farm Shop
FRESH RICOTTA MALFATTI WITH SAGE BUTTER

The trick with this recipe is to make the homemade ricotta using raw unpasteurised milk (for example, the raw milk sold in Welbeck Farm Shop, sourced from Collingthwaite Dairy) as it hasn't been homogenised and so creates a rich and creamy cheese. Joe Parente developed this dish from two recipes in his friends' cookbooks, which has become his children's favourite!

Preparation time: 15 minutes | Cooking time: 15 minutes | Serves 4-5 as a starter

Ingredients

For the homemade ricotta:

2.25 litres (4 pints) raw milk

¼ tsp salt

40ml white vinegar

For the malfatti:

250g spinach

250g homemade ricotta

50g Parmesan

1 large egg

40g plain or Italian 00 flour, plus plenty for rolling

Pinch nutmeg, grated

24 sage leaves

75g butter

Method

First, make your ricotta. Shop-bought ricotta can be used for this recipe but for the best taste and freshness, it's simple to make your own. The finished cheese will be fine in a sealed container in the fridge for a few days, but is at its best almost immediately after making.

Pour the milk into a large non-reactive pan, add the salt and place over a medium heat. Gently heat the milk, giving it an occasional stir, until it starts steaming and the smallest bubbles appear. At this point, check the temperature with a thermometer – the milk should reach around 82-85°c. Remove from the heat, add the vinegar and stir gently. You'll begin to see curds starting to form so continue to stir for another minute or so. Cover with a clean cloth and let the mixture sit for a couple of hours to cool. Once it's rested, spoon the ricotta into a colander lined with a damp muslin and allow to drain for an hour or so, and then decant into a sealable container to be kept in the fridge until use.

For the malfatti, boil the spinach in salted water until tender and then refresh under cold water to keep the vibrant colour. Squeeze as much moisture out of the spinach as possible, then chop it very finely. Mix the chopped spinach with 250g of the homemade ricotta, Parmesan, egg, flour and nutmeg to form a soft dough.

Bring a pan of salted water to the boil and then begin to shape the malfatti. Drop a walnut-sized lump of dough onto a bed of flour and roll into a rough ball. Don't worry if the dough is a little too soft to make a perfect ball (the name Malfatti means 'badly formed'!) but check that it will hold together by cooking the first one in the boiling water. If it doesn't, add a bit more flour into the mixture and try again.

Once the dough is just (but only just) firm enough to withstand cooking, roll the remainder into a dozen or so golf ball size pieces, coating them in plenty of flour, and simmer for 7-8 minutes, timing from when the balls rise to the surface.

To serve

While they're cooking, fry the sage in the butter until the leaves are crisp and the butter has turned nutty, brown and foamy. Carefully remove the malfatti from the pan which should be just oozing in the middle, drain and serve drizzled with the sage butter and the crispy sage leaves on top. I also occasionally serve these with a homemade tomato sauce and a sprinkle more Parmesan for a lovely light meal or starter.

Lessons in
ARTISAN FOOD

The School of Artisan Food is tucked away on the Welbeck Estate in Nottinghamshire, offering short courses and an advanced diploma to bring long-forgotten, traditional methods of food production back to life with enthusiasm and expertise.

Alison Swan Parente founded The School of Artisan Food in 2009, a year after she set up The Welbeck Bakehouse, to reintroduce a traditional, high-quality bread-making culture into the county. The School became the perfect place for the bakers to hone their skills, and soon expanded beyond baking to include the crafts of butchery, cheesemaking, fermentation and preserving, foraging, patisserie, and more.

The wide range of specialist short courses is open to everyone from keen amateurs to professionals, and can be just half a day or up to four weeks depending on what you choose. The School of Artisan Food places great emphasis on traditional food production skills that could have been lost had they not been reignited and passed on by the talented tutors, cherry-picked from working professionals at the top of their game, to their enthusiastic and diverse mix of students. The School is highly regarded within the artisanal food community and not just at Welbeck – tutors regularly see people from the industry joining their courses to upskill and improve their practice.

For those with the ambition and drive to become professional bakers, at whatever stage in their life, The School offers a full-time Advanced Diploma in Artisan Baking taught by experts, which equips its graduates with the skills to operate in the 'real world' – alumni include Sophie Wood who founded the handmade baked snack company Barmies, as well as other practicing bakers and business owners across the UK and Europe. If you already have an artisan food concept but haven't quite found your business acumen, there are increasingly popular food business start-up courses that give students the guidance, confidence and know-how to start up their own foodie venture.

The building itself is extensive, with a library, lecture theatre, three professional training rooms, a common room and a refectory – the latter is where everyone gathers for a 'school dinner' freshly cooked and served up by the chefs so that staff, students and tutors alike can enjoy a bit of downtime together over a great meal. The School of Artisan Food is a registered charity and not-for profit organisation and works closely with other charities and local suppliers, such as a nearby social enterprise Rhubarb Farm, and its courses promote sustainable practices which can be embraced at home. No longer forgotten, the skills taught here are invaluable to anyone interested in food heritage, or simply in great tasting homemade food.

The School of Artisan Food
HERDWICK MUTTON CURRY

This delicious curry has warmth but not fiery heat; Wayne Caddy's naan bread recipe, plus a crispy pakora or two on the side, makes this a brilliant comfort food dish.

Preparation time: 1 hour, plus proving & fermentation | Cooking time: 1 hour | Serves 4-6

Ingredients

For the curry:

500g diced mutton (Herdwick mutton for the best flavour)

1 large white onion, diced

Splash of oil and knob of butter

1 tsp each of garam masala, cayenne pepper, turmeric, ground pepper and ground cumin

Large pinch of salt

1 large sweet potato, diced

100g fresh ginger, finely diced

1 x 400g tin chopped tomatoes

2 tbsp tomato purée

1 tin coconut milk

For the onion pakoras:

4 large onions, finely sliced

1 tbsp salt

1½ tbsp ground cumin

1 tbsp each of ground coriander, chilli powder and turmeric

Half a bunch of fresh coriander, chopped

1 garlic clove, finely chopped

1 tbsp ginger, finely chopped

Vegetable oil, to deep fry

Gram flour

For the naan breads:

150g organic bread flour

90g water

350g organic bread flour

5g yeast

25g yoghurt

9g salt

20g ghee or butter

200g milk

5g black onion seeds

3g cumin

Method

Brown off the mutton with a little oil in a pan over a medium-high heat, and set aside. In the same pan, gently fry the diced onions in oil and butter until translucent. Add the salt and all of the spices, ensuring they don't catch and burn, then return the mutton to the pan and add the diced sweet potato and ginger. Once the sweet potato has some colour, add the chopped tomatoes, tomato purée and coconut milk. Bring to the boil, then turn down to the lowest heat and let everything reduce. The longer it cooks, the thicker and tastier it will get. Ideally, prepare the curry the night before and let it stew overnight, covered but with no heat.

To make the naan breads, start by making a ferment the night before. Make sure the water is at room temperature (about 18c) and sprinkle in the yeast. Add the bread flour and mix until the dough comes together. Cover and leave to ferment overnight (at least 12 hours) at room temperature.

To make the onion pakoras, place the onions and salt into a large bowl. Mix well and allow to stand for 5-10 minutes. Add all of the spices, garlic, ginger and half of the fresh coriander including the stalks if you wish. Mix everything well with your hands. Add the gram flour a tablespoon at a time until a batter forms that lightly coats the onion slices. Now heat the vegetable oil in a deep frying pan. When the oil is hot enough, use two forks to pick up a small amount of the mix and slowly place it into the oil. For a light and crunchy pakora, use the forks to gently tease the mix apart whilst in the oil. Fry each pakora until golden in colour.

For the naan breads, mix all the ingredients together by hand, including the ferment. The dough should look soft but have elasticity. Leave to prove for 2 hours. Next, preheat the oven to the highest temperature setting. Handling the dough gently, divide it into 8 even balls, and stretch each ball into a rounded teardrop shape by hand. Bake in batches in the preheated oven until you see slightly charred bubbles on the surface, this won't take long so watch them carefully!

To serve

Gently reheat the mutton curry until piping hot throughout, then place a few generous spoonfuls into a bowl alongside some fluffy basmati rice. Place one or two pakoras on the side plus a hot, freshly baked naan bread for each person. Tuck in!

One night in
BANGKOK

Zaap Thai is the place to go for fresh, authentic street food representing all the provinces of Thailand – you'll be transported to the city's bustling markets without having left Nottingham!

An evening out at Nottingham's Zaap Thai is about immersion in Thai culture as much as the freshly prepared, aromatic food. The Thai way of eating embraces all dishes at the same time, as opposed to a more structured mealtime, as we do in the UK. So, Zaap encourages customers to pick and choose from starters, mains, snacks and sides, and enjoy them all together. Especially, if you have people to share the food with!

Zaap's bright and colourful décor can't help but generate excitement, with all the adornments imported from Thailand to preserve the authenticity, which is so important to the Zaap team.

Head chef and owner, Ban Kaewkraikhot, was born in Thailand, and food was always a big part of her family life. Ban always helped her mum to make the evening meal after coming home from school or work each day. When she moved to the UK, Ban wanted to recreate the freshness and intense flavours of her mum's food, and to share her enjoyment of cooking it with others.

May 2015 saw the opening of her first Zaap restaurant in Leeds, followed closely by the Nottingham Zaap in November of the same year. This venue, located between Maid Marian Way and the Market Square, has become the busiest of all of them thanks to plenty of enthusiastic local custom!

With lots of space for groups, this is the only Zaap that takes bookings. It's popular with all sorts of customers, from young professionals out for lunch, to families whose children love the reconstruction of a traditional Thai railway station, complete with model engine and train tracks running across the floor. The atmosphere is fun and casual, whilst the service is speedy but friendly, and the food is made to please – Zaap lets you choose your spice level, from 'safe to Zaap' to keep everyone's taste buds happy!

Owner Ban never fails to find a great sense of satisfaction when she sees people enjoying her food, and her longstanding passion for recreating the authentic flavours of her home lends itself to a unique dining experience in the heart of the city.

Zaap Thai
PAD GA PRAO MOO (STIR-FRIED CHILLI AND BASIL MINCED PORK)

Bird's eye chillies are also known as Thai chillies, come in red or green varieties and are very, very hot! Combined with garlic, soy sauce, oyster sauce and sugar, they infuse the pork with a beautifully balanced salty, sweet heat.

Preparation time: 5 minutes | Cooking time: approx. 20 minutes | Serves 1

Ingredients

200g minced pork

2 tbsp vegetable oil

1 tbsp garlic, finely chopped

2 tbsp bird's eye chilli, finely chopped

1 red chilli, sliced and deseeded

2 tbsp oyster sauce

½ tsp sugar

30g basil leaves

10g fine beans, cut into 2 inch pieces

1 tbsp light soy sauce

Splash of water

Method

Heat the oil in a wok over a medium heat, then add the finely chopped bird's eye chilli and garlic, and allow to sweat a little. Add the minced pork, breaking it up with a spoon and stirring often so the chilli and garlic don't burn.

Once the minced pork is cooked, add the fine beans and stir them into the mixture. Add the oyster sauce, sugar, light soy sauce and a splash of water, stir and then taste.

The basil and red chilli go in at the last minute. Stir them through and then serve the dish straightaway. We recommend pairing our Pad Ga Prao Moo with jasmine rice and a fried egg – sunny side up.

The DIRECTORY

These great businesses have supported the making of this book; please support and enjoy them.

200 Degrees Coffee Roasters
16 Flying Horse Walk
Nottingham
NG1 2HN
Telephone: 0115 837 3150
Website: www.200degs.com

200 Degrees Coffee Roasters
99 Carrington Street
Nottingham
NG1 7FE
Telephone: 0115 837 2240
Website: www.200degs.com
Artisan coffee roasters with two distinctive coffee shops in Nottingham that serve breakfasts, fresh sandwiches and cakes alongside their delicious house blend and weekly guest single origin coffees.

Alchemilla
192 Derby Road
Nottingham
NG7 1NF
Telephone: 0115 941 3515
Website: www.alchemillarestaurant.uk
Brand new restaurant in Nottingham serving contemporary cuisine, brought to you by Alex Bond.

Angel Microbrewery
7 Stoney Street
Nottingham
NG1 1LG
Telephone: 0115 9483343
Website: www.angelmicrobrewery.com
Freehouse and microbrewery steeped in history with a food menu for herbivores and carnivores alike, regular gigs, and a bar featuring local vegan ales plus one or two of the brewery's own beers.

Annie's Burger Shack
5 Broadway
Lace Market
Nottingham
NG1 1PR
Telephone: 0115 684 9920
Website: www.anniesburgershack.com
Authentic American dining experience with a menu featuring more than 30 burger inventions as well as breakfasts inspired by the four corners of the US.

The Bakehouse
631-633 Mansfield Road
Nottingham
NG5 2FX
Telephone: 0115 956 9430
Email:
thebakehousenotts@outlook.com
Award-winning bakery, café and micro-pub The Bakehouse is run by husband and wife team Craig and Rosea Poynter, whose commitment to community engagement and top-quality produce has made them a fixture of the Nottinghamshire food scene.

Bar Iberico
17-19 Carlton Street
Nottingham
NG1 1NL
Telephone: 0115 9881133
Website: www.baribericotapas.com
All day tapas bar focusing on classic Spanish flavours, with three beautifully designed areas in which to enjoy the food, drink and easy going atmosphere.

The Black Bull at Blidworth
Main Street
Blidworth
Mansfield
NG21 0QH
Telephone: 01623 490222
Website:
www.blackbullblidworth.co.uk
Close to Sherwood Forest and surrounded by beautiful Nottinghamshire countryside, The Black Bull at Blidworth offers an eclectic, seasonally-inspired menu alongside stylish, characterful B&B rooms in a beautiful 18th century building.

Blend
Unit 30, Avenue C
Sneinton Market
Nottingham
NG1 1DW
Telephone: 0115 838950
Website: www.blendnottingham.co.uk
Stewarts and Blend are two halves of a coffee-lovers paradise, as Stewarts roast the coffee and Blend serves it next door alongside a host of pastries, cakes, and grilled cheese sandwiches in a cafe designed to bring people together with a relaxed and friendly atmosphere.

Bluebird Tea Co.
5 Victoria Street
Nottingham
NG1 2EW
Website: www.bluebirdteaco.com
Brand new store selling award-winning loose leaf tea blends and spreading happiness with every sip, from the independent mixologists leading the way in UK tea innovation.

Cartwheel Café and Roastery
16 Low Pavement
Nottingham
NG1 7DL
Telephone: 0115 959 8434
Website: www.cartwheelcoffee.com
The café serves fresh coffee, served how you like it, straight from the roastery alongside a menu of quality brunch dishes, sandwiches and cakes all made in-house by the head chef.

The Cheese Shop
6 Flying Horse Walk
St Peters Gate
Nottingham
NG1 2HN
Telephone: 0115 941 9114
Website:
www.cheeseshop-nottingham.co.uk
Brothers Rob and Webb have run the shop for over 15 years and are experts when it comes to sourcing artisan cheeses from the UK and beyond to sell in their shop and licensed café.

The Clock House Café & Tea Room
Upton Hall
Main Street
Upton
Nottinghamshire
NG23 5TE
Telephone: 01636 919591
Website: www.clockhousecafe.co.uk
Café and tea room with charming vintage décor serving freshly baked scones and cakes, as well as breakfasts and main meals using local produce. The venue is also available for private hire with event catering.

The Cod's Scallops
170 Bramcote Lane
Wollaton
Nottingham
NG8 2PQ
Telephone: 0115 985 4107
Website: www.codsscallops.com

The Cod's Scallops
311-313 Mansfield Road
Nottingham
NG5 2DA
Telephone: 0115 708 0251
Website: www.codsscallops.com
Not just your ordinary fish and chips – The Cod's Scallops serves the freshest seafood to eat in and takeaway as well as selling the daily catch on a wet fish counter. Long Eaton – coming soon!

Colston Bassett Dairy Ltd.
Harby Lane
Colston Bassett
Nottingham
NG12 3FN
Telephone: 01949 81322
Website:
www.colstonbassettdairy.co.uk
This multi-award winning dairy creates rich, creamy Blue Stilton and Shropshire Blue cheeses using traditional methods gleaned from its 100-year heritage.

Copper Cafés
27-33 Market Street
Nottingham
NG1 6HX
Telephone: 0115 985 9304
Website: www.coppercafe.co.uk

Copper Cafés
21-23 Central Avenue
West Bridgford
Nottingham
NG2 5GQ
Telephone: 0115 981 4254
Website: www.coppercafe.co.uk

Copper Cafés
930 Woodborough Road
Mapperley
Nottingham
NG3 5QS
Telephone: 0115 960 9259
Website: www.coppercafe.co.uk
With three stylish venues that move effortlessly from relaxed daytime cafés to comfortable evening lounge bars, Copper Cafés offer high quality food and drink accompanied by friendly service in popular locations.

Debbie Bryan
18 St Mary's Gate
The Lace Market
Nottingham
NG1 1PF
Telephone: 0115 9507776
Website: www.debbiebryan.co.uk
A unique Nottingham venture offering crafting opportunities and events that celebrate the city's heritage alongside a welcoming tea room and gift shop full of beautiful handmade products.

Edward's
142 Wollaton Road
Beeston
Nottingham
NG9 2PE
Telephone: 0115 9226309
Website: www.danbycatering.com
Adventurous, theatrical street food restaurant with emphasis on the dining experience as a whole, including breakfast, daytime and 8 course tasting menus featuring international flavours.

Forty Four Bridgford Cocktail Bar and Kitchen
44 Bridgford Road
West Bridgford
Nottingham
NG2 6AP
Telephone: 0115 784 4799
Website: www.fortyfourbridgford.co.uk
Serving food from 10am in a relaxed daytime atmosphere and fabulous cocktails all evening, Forty Four Bridgford is a family-run bar and kitchen that invites you to eat, drink and party with them!

Fred Hallam Ltd.
23 High Road
Beeston
Nottingham
NG9 2JQ
Telephone: 0115 9254 766
Website: www.fredhallam.com
Family-run fishmonger and greengrocer in Beeston, which has supplied expert knowledge along with fresh fish, fruit, vegetables and dairy products wholesale and locally for over 100 years.

Freshly Spiced
Carlton
Nottingham
Telephone: 07468 269109
Website: www.freshlyspiced.co.uk
Freshly Spiced create spice blends and recipe kits from fresh whole ingredients to add wonderful natural flavour to home-cooked food. The website is full of recipe ideas and spicy hints and tips.

The Frustrated Chef
90-94 Chilwell Road
Beeston
Nottingham
NG9 1ES
Telephone: 0115 922 8300
Website: www.thefrustratedchef.co.uk
A relatively new but popular addition to Beeston's restaurant scene, serving world tapas in a contemporary setting with a focus on authenticity and originality in every freshly-made dish.

George's Great British Kitchen
Queens Street
Nottingham
NG1 2BL
Telephone: 0115 950 5521
Website:
www.georgesgreatbritishkitchen.co.uk
Serving British classics with unique twists, in a beautifully designed restaurant where as much attention has been paid to the décor as to the food, with a touch of nostalgia and stylish charm.

Gurkha One
Staythorpe Road
Rolleston
Newark
Nottingham
NG23 5SG
Telephone: 01636 819000
Website: www.gurkha-one.co.uk
Restaurant serving authentic Indian and Nepalese cuisine where booking in advance is strongly recommended due to popularity. There is also a bar area serving real ale with a traditional pub feel in this quiet, welcoming village location.

Homeboys
We have fixed premises at Nottingham Street Food Club:
Clock Tower Dining Food Court
INTU Victoria Centre
222 Victoria Street
Nottingham NG1 3PT
Email: hi@homeboys.com
Contemporary Asian street food from Masterchef finalist Pete Hewitt. Served from a restored 1978 American Step Van, both on the road across the UK and at Nottingham Street Food Club.

Homemade
Hockley
20 Pelham Street
Nottingham
NG1 2EG
Telephone: 0115 924 3030
Website: www.homemadecafe.com

Homemade
Pavilion, Forest Rec.
Forest Recreation Ground Pavilion
Mansfield Road
Nottingham
NG5 2BU
Telephone: 0115 978 1608
Website: www.homemadecafe.com
Two beautiful locations with unique atmospheres serving locally sourced, homemade goodness, with catering options for events and cakes to order.

MemSaab
12-14 Maid Marian Way
Nottingham
NG1 6HS
Telephone: 0115 957 0009
Website: www.mem-saab.co.uk
Fine dining Indian restaurant with stylish interior and à la carte menu cooked by chefs with specialist regional knowledge, reflecting Indian cuisine from the traditional to the very modern.

Mr & Mrs Fine Wine
The Wine Bank
Church Street
Southwell
Nottinghamshire
NG25 0HD
Telephone: 01636 918182
Website:
www.mrandmrsfinewine.co.uk
An independent wine merchant in Southwell providing friendly and knowledgeable advice, with a schedule of fun events and over 450 handpicked wines, spirits, beers and liqueurs to choose from in the relaxed environment of the shop and bar.

Mulberry Tree Café
Strelley Hall
Main Street
Strelley Village
Nottingham
NG8 6PE
Telephone: 0115 906 1305 / 1200 (office)
Website:
www.mulberrytreestrelley.co.uk
Mulberry Tree Café is an idyllic spot for a relaxing lunch or a small treat from the menu of home cooked food, with a large choice of loose leaf teas. Perfect for walkers or cyclists, but close to the city too – a real hidden gem.

Ottar Chocolate
Brewery Yard
Telephone: 01909 512 579
Website: www.ottarchocolate.com
Award-winning team of chocolatiers and pastry chefs, creating botanically-inspired flavours from completely natural ingredients, with a focus on ethical sourcing.

The Railway Lowdham
Station Road
Lowdham
Nottinghamshire
NG14 7DU
Telephone: 0115 966 3222
Website: www.railwaylowdham.co.uk
A village pub to shout about, The Railway Lowdham offers a straightforward yet creative menu, fantastic wine and gin lists, real ales, cosy fires and a unique interior to welcome all comers.

The Rustic Crust
Telephone: 07977 288150
Website: www.therusticcrust.co.uk
Authentic Neapolitan-style pizza made fresh to order and served out of Poppy, a converted Land Rover housing a wood-fired Italian oven, for any occasion all over the UK.

Sauce Shop
Telephone: 0115 9413 263
Website: www.sauce-shop.co.uk
Producers of handmade craft sauces, made with real ingredients to create delicious accompaniments to a range of foods. Based in Nottingham with over 250 stockists across the UK.

Spring Lane Farm Shop

Mapperley Plains

Nottingham

NG3 5RQ

Telephone: 0115 926 7624

Website:

www.springlanefarmshop.co.uk

Recently renovated farm shop with onsite butchery and bakery, stocking the farm's own beef, potatoes, and baked goods as well as a deli counter, fruit and vegetables, preserves, dairy and more.

Starkey's Fruit

Norwood Park

Southwell

Nottinghamshire

NG25 0PF

Telephone: 01636 819454

Website: www.johnstarkey.co

Starkey's Fruit is a supplier of top-quality apples and soft fruit, as well as delicious juices and compote created on the premises. Starkey's signature product is the famous Bramley apple, grown in the only commercial orchard of original variety Bramley apples.

Stewarts of Trent Bridge

Unit 31, Avenue C

Sneinton Market

Nottingham

NG1 1DW

Telephone: 0115 8990610

Website: www.stewartscoffees.co.uk

Stewarts and Blend are two halves of a coffee-lovers paradise, as Stewarts roast the coffee and Blend serves it next door alongside a host of pastries, cakes, and grilled cheese sandwiches in a cafe designed to bring people together with a relaxed and friendly atmosphere.

Thaymar Ice Cream, Farm Shop & Tea Room

Haughton Park Farm

Near Bothamsall

Retford

Nottinghamshire

DN22 8DB

Telephone: 01623 862632

Website: www.thaymaricecream.co.uk

Thaymar offers over 35 flavours of award-winning luxury ice cream and sorbet all made on site with natural ingredients, as well as fresh produce in the farm shop, and a renowned tea room whose menu features the farm's own beef and lamb.

Tiffin Teahouse

35 Abbey Road

West Bridgford

Nottingham

NG2 5NG

Telephone: 0115 981 6224

Website: www.tiffinteahouse.uk.com

Offering a delicate slice of nostalgia alongside their afternoon teas and traditional lunch and breakfast menus, Tiffin Teahouse focus on fresh, tasty, homemade food for customers of all ages.

Tipsy T

908 Woodborough Road

Mapperley

Nottingham

NG3 5QR

Telephone: 0115 956 9495

Website: www.tipsyt.co.uk

Friendly, independent café bar on Mapperley Top serving a traditional tea room menu throughout the day and transforming into a relaxed evening venue with cocktails, beers and a range of over 140 gins, which are also served at regular tasting events.

Toast

202 Derby Road

Nottingham

NG7 1NQ

Telephone: 0115 837 1890

Website: www.toastnottingham.co.uk

Welcoming café and deli with a fantastic range of produce, much of it local, including meats, cheese, cakes, gifts, cards, wine, beer, tea and coffee, plus bookable event space.

Victoria Market

Glasshouse Street

Nottingham

NG1 3LP

Telephone: 0115 876 1960

Website:

www.nottinghamcity.gov.uk/markets

The only indoor market in Nottingham and a hub of the community, Victoria Market sells everything from plants to mushy peas, haberdashery to ice cream and is a great place to meet and shop.

Visit Nottinghamshire

Telephone: 0844 477 5678

Website:

www.visit-nottinghamshire.co.uk

Contact Nottingham Tourist Information Centre for ideas and information on food and drink, events, activities and things to do in Nottinghamshire, and to help you plan your visit.

Vork Pie

Telephone: 07810 013435

Website: www.vorkpie.co.uk

Sophie Neill runs the pie-eyed kitchen, developing 100% vegan creations including pies and Scotch eggs which can be found at local markets as well as in several Nottingham pubs and cafés.

The Welbeck Estate

Welbeck
Worksop
Nottinghamshire
S80 3LW

A traditional landed estate in a beautiful rural location, boasting an award-winning farm shop, brewery, chocolatier, bakehouse and The School of Artisan Food.

Ottar Chocolate

Brewery Yard
Telephone: 01909 512 579
Website: www.ottarchocolate.com

Award-winning team of chocolatiers and pastry chefs, creating botanically-inspired flavours from completely natural ingredients, with a focus on ethical sourcing.

The School of Artisan Food

Lower Motor Yard
Telephone: 01909 532 171
Website: www.schoolofartisanfood.org

School with an outstanding reputation, dedicated to teaching skills based around sustainable and traditional methods of food production.

Welbeck Abbey Brewery

Brewery Yard
Telephone: 01909 512 539
Website: www.welbeckabbeybrewery.co.uk

Microbrewery using traditional methods to create a fantastic range of beer and real ale on the estate grounds. Tours of the brewery by appointment only.

The Welbeck Bakehouse

Lower Motor Yard
Telephone: 01909 500 129
Website: www.welbeckbakehouse.co.uk

Bakery specialising in sourdough and Viennoiserie, using traditional fermentation methods to produce an incredible range of artisanal bread and pastries.

Welbeck Farm Shop

The Courtyard
Telephone: 01909 478 725
Website: www.welbeckfarmshop.co.uk

One of the country's best farm shops, with a focus on low food miles and artisanal produce. Two-thirds of the impressive product range is from the Welbeck estate, including Ottar Chocolate, Welbeck Abbey Brewery and Welbeck Bakehouse.

Zaap Thai

Unit B
Bromely Place
Nottingham
NG1 6JG
Telephone: 0115 947 0204
Website: www.zaapthai.co.uk

Authentic Thai street food served in a venue designed to transport you straight to a bustling Bangkok food market in the heart of Nottingham.

INDEX

S

T

V

W

Y

Other titles in the 'Get Stuck In' series

The Essex Cook Book features Thomas Leatherbarrow, The Anchor Riverside, Great Garnetts, Deersbrook Farm, Mayfield Bakery and lots more.
978-1-910863-25-1

The South London Cook Book features Jose Pizarro, Adam Byatt, The Alma, Piccalilli Caff, Canopy Beer, Inkspot Brewery and lots more.
978-1-910863-27-5

The Brighton & Sussex Cook Book features Steven Edwards, The Bluebird Tea Co, Isaac At, Real Patisserie, Sussex Produce Co, and lots more.
978-1-910863-22-0

The Oxfordshire Cook Book features Mike North of The Nut Tree Inn, Sudbury House, Jacobs Inn, The Muddy Duck and lots more.
978-1-910863-08-4

The Lancashire Cook Book features Andrew Nutter of Nutters Restaurant, Bertram's, The Blue Mallard and lots more.
978-1-910863-09-1

The Liverpool Cook Book features Burnt Truffle, The Art School, Fraiche, Villaggio Cucina and many more.
978-1-910863-15-2

The Sheffield Cook Book - Second Helpings features Jameson's Tea Rooms, Craft & Dough, The Wortley Arms, The Holt, Grind Café and lots more.
978-1-910863-16-9

The Leeds Cook Book features The Boxtree, Crafthouse, Stockdales of Yorkshire and lots more.
978-1-910863-18-3

The Cotswolds Cook Book features David Everitt-Matthias of Champignon Sauvage, Prithvi, Chef's Dozen and lots more.
978-0-9928981-9-9

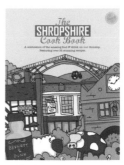

The Shropshire Cook Book features Chris Burt of The Peach Tree, Old Downton Lodge, Shrewsbury Market, CSons and lots more.
978-1-910863-32-9

The Norfolk Cook Book features Richard Bainbridge, Morston Hall, The Duck Inn and lots more.
978-1-910863-01-5

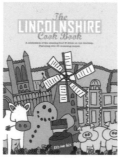

The Lincolnshire Cook Book features Colin McGurran of Winteringham Fields, TV chef Rachel Green, San Pietro and lots more.
978-1-910863-05-3

The Bristol Cook Book features Dean Edwards, Lido, Clifton Sausage, The Ox, and wines from Corks of Cotham plus lots more.
978-1-910863-14-5

The Cheshire Cook Book features Simon Radley of The Chester Grosvenor, The Chef's Table, Great North Pie Co., Harthill Cookery School and lots more.
978-1-910863-07-7

The Leicestershire & Rutland Cook Book features Tim Hart of Hambleton Hall, John's House, Farndon Fields, Leicester Market, Walter Smith and lots more.
978-0-9928981-8-2

All books in this series are available from Waterstones, Amazon and independent bookshops.

FIND OUT MORE ABOUT US AT WWW.MEZEPUBLISHING.CO.UK